ANIMAL TRACKS
ACTIVITY BOOK

by Brett Ortler,
illustrations by Shane Nitzsche, Anna Christenson,
Julie Martinez and Bruce Wilson

To my nature trackers: Oliver, Violet and Charlie,
and their furry assistants, Bullwinkle, Truffles
and Peanut.

~Brett

D1362282

Cover design by Jonathan Norberg
Book design by Lora Westberg

10 9 8 7 6 5 4

Copyright © 2015 by Brett Ortler
Published by Adventure Publications
An imprint of AdventureKEEN
330 Garfield Street South
Cambridge, Minnesota 55008
(800) 678-7006
www.adventurepublications.net
All rights reserved
Printed in U.S.A.
ISBN 978-1-59193-538-4 (pbk.)

Author's Note: This book is a general introduction to the world of tracking. When you're trying to identify a track, be sure to bring along an adult and a field guide. Also, note that animal tracks in this book are not always shown to scale; the track illustrations are intended to give you a rough idea of the shape and layout of a track in order to help you to learn more. (Because not all tracks show up in their entirety, we sometimes add an outline to show you the general shape of an animal's foot.)

What is Tracking?

Have you ever found an animal track in the mud or snow? Then you're an animal tracker! Animal tracking was once a very important skill; people depended on tracking to find food, learn about the landscape and even to know whether dangerous animals were in the area.

Today, we don't depend on tracking to find our food, but tracking is a great way to get outside, learn about nature and discover what animals live in your area.

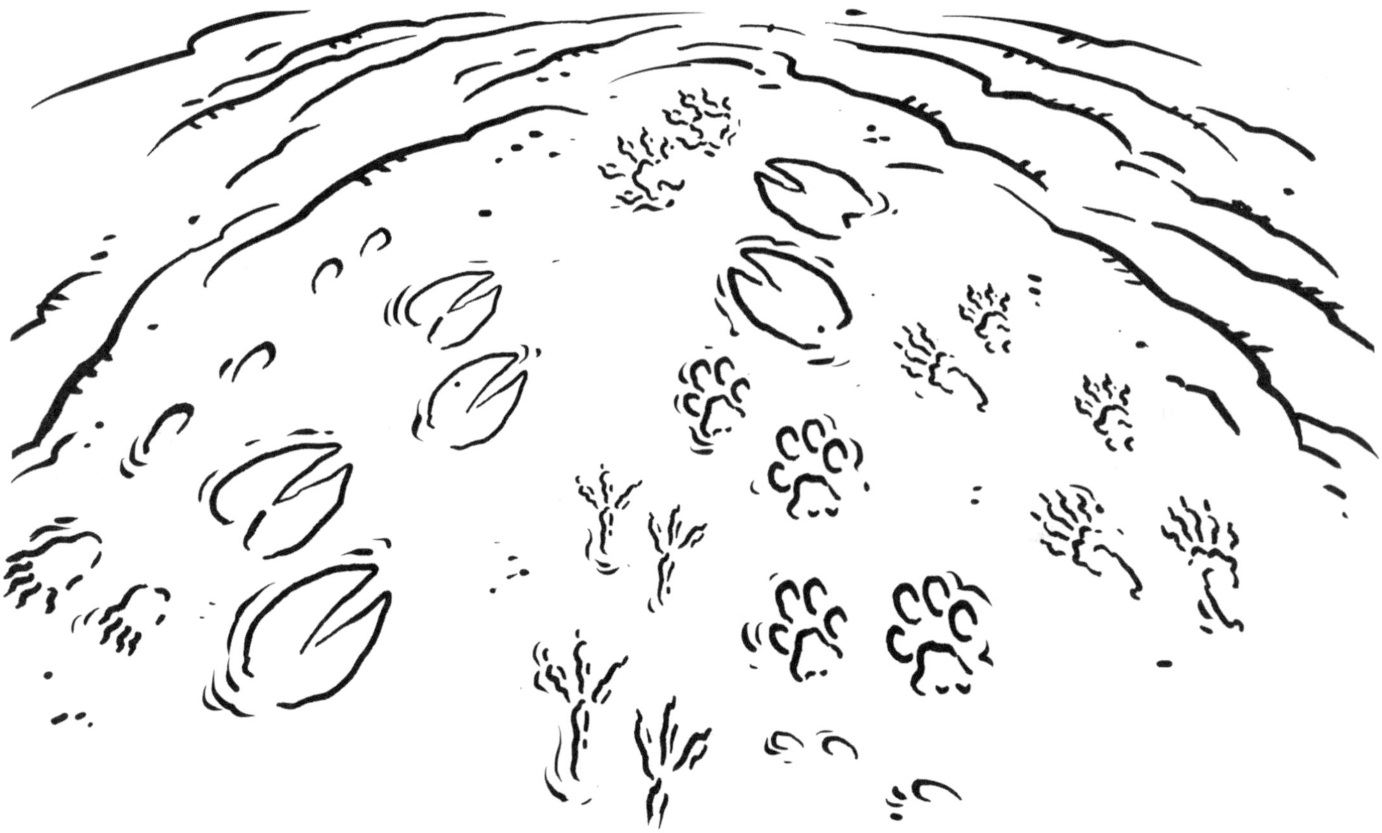

You don't need to visit the wilderness to find animal tracks. You might even find them in your yard!

Looking at a Track

The first step to identifying an animal track is to look at it closely. The following simple questions can help you learn more about the animal that made a track.

1. What shape and size is the track?

The first thing to notice is the track's shape and size. This tells you a lot about the animal that made it. Is it heart-shaped and huge? Tiny and hand-like? In addition, animals that are related (white-tailed deer and elk, for instance) have tracks with similar shapes, so if you can recognize the shape, it can help you figure out what kind of animal made the track.

2. Count the number of toes and look for claw marks

Believe it or not, not all animals have the same number of toes! When you find a track, count how many toes the front and rear tracks have, as this will help you narrow down the possibilities.

When you're counting the toes, be sure to look for claw marks. Some animals have claws, but others don't. Not all claws look the same. Some animals leave claw marks that are easy to see, but in other tracks, claw marks are harder to see or may not show up at all.

3. Measure the track and ask an adult for help

Measure the track (see page 4 for instructions), and ask an adult to help you find the track in an Animal Tracks field guide. See page 61 for a list of recommended books.

4. Look around!

Where you find a track can be just as important as the track itself, as it tells you where an animal lives. This can help narrow down the options, making it easier to identify a track.

Can you guess the track shown above? See page 62 for the answer?

Measuring Tracks

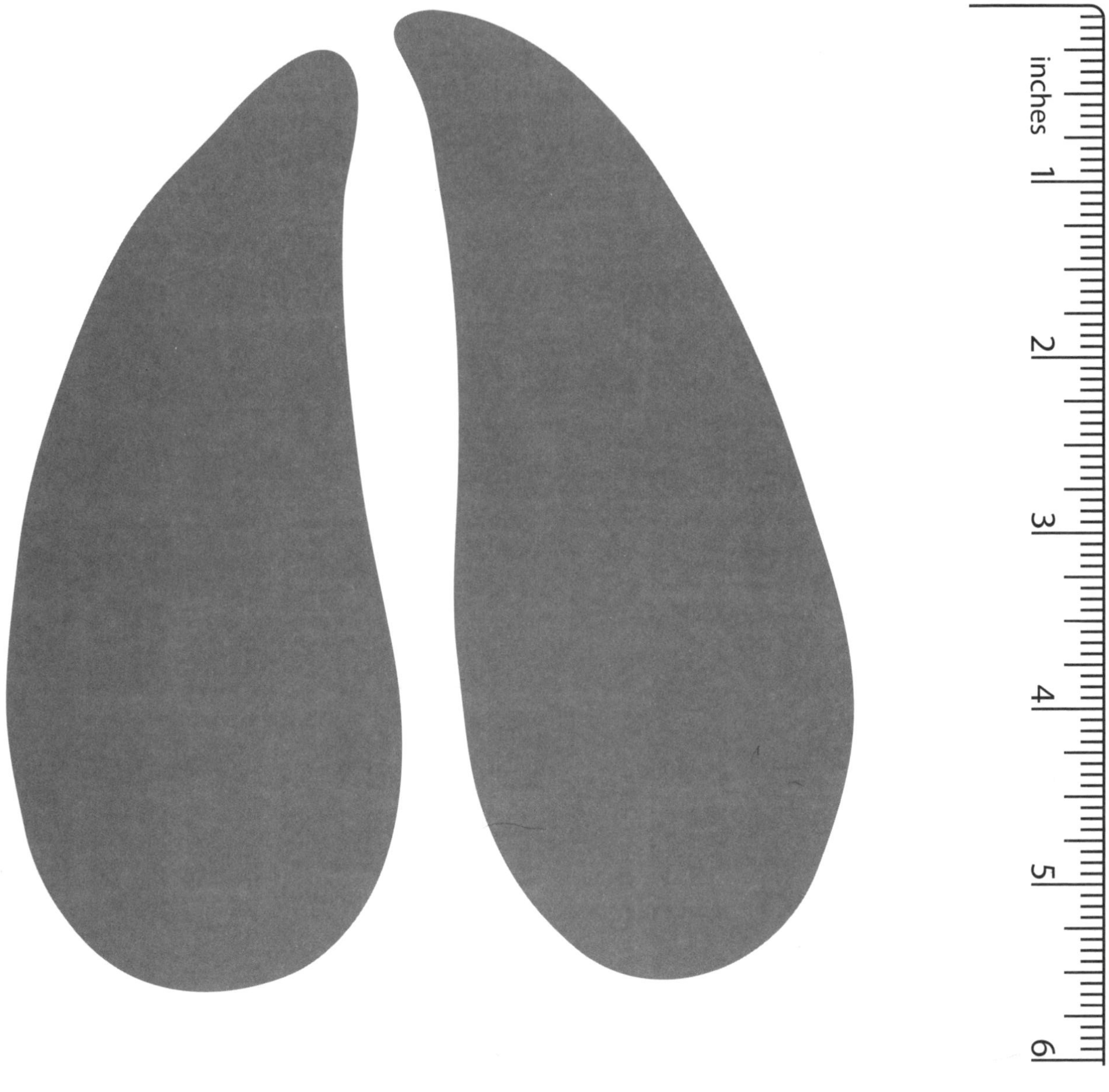

inches
1
2
3
4
5
6

Measuring tracks is a great way to make yourself look closely at a track. When measuring, start from the bottom of the track and measure to the top. Then measure the track at its widest point. When measuring, don't include claw marks. Measure the track shown above. What did you come up with?

Keep in mind that the type of ground a track is made in (sand, dirt, snow) can change the size of a track.

Pads and Claws

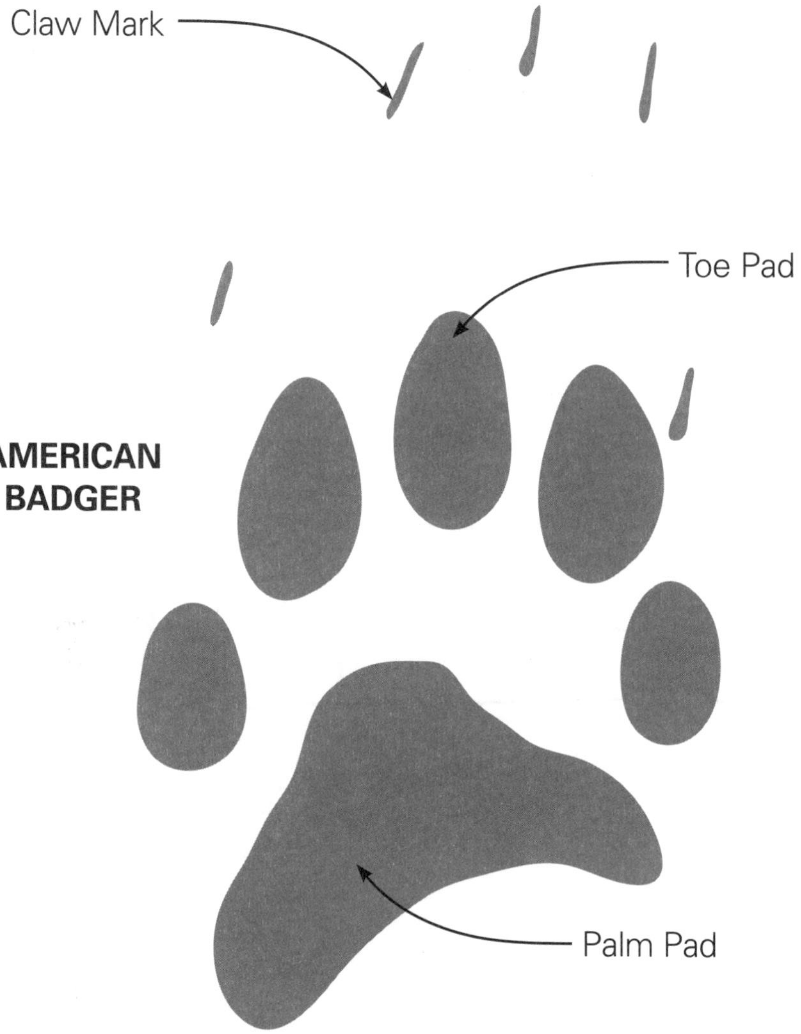

Claw Mark

Toe Pad

AMERICAN
BADGER

Palm Pad

HOUSE CAT

GRAY WOLF

COUGAR

When you find a track, look for claw and pad marks; these marks are left behind by some animals' feet or toes. There are two types of pads. The central part of an animal's foot is called a palm pad; toe pads leave marks, too. Noting the presence (or absence) of pads/claws helps you rule out possibilities.

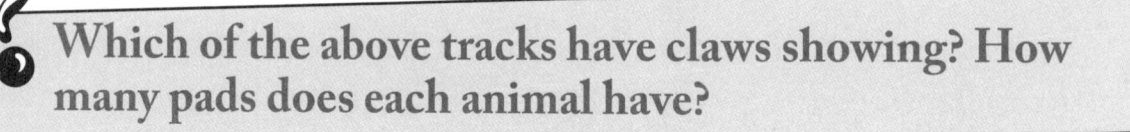

Which of the above tracks have claws showing? How many pads does each animal have?

Animal Signs

Animals don't just leave footprints behind. They leave all sorts of other clues, called signs. Examples include hair, chewed-up vegetation and more. Some animals, such as beavers, even build dams and lodges! When you find a track, see if you can find other clues!

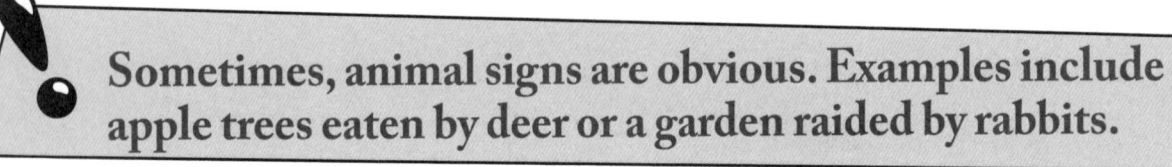

Sometimes, animal signs are obvious. Examples include apple trees eaten by deer or a garden raided by rabbits.

Animal Scat

BEAR SCAT

HOUSE MOUSE SCAT

DEER SCAT

Animals leave something else behind: poop! Scientists have another name for animal poop: scat. While it might seem gross, each animal's scat looks a little different, so if you spot some, it can help you figure out which animal was in the area.

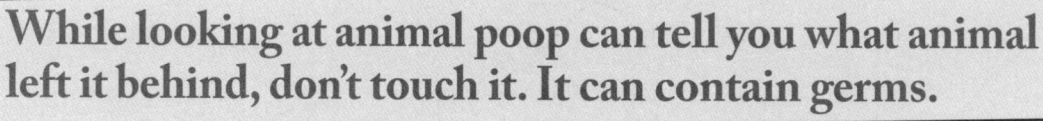

While looking at animal poop can tell you what animal left it behind, don't touch it. It can contain germs.

Animal Names Word Find

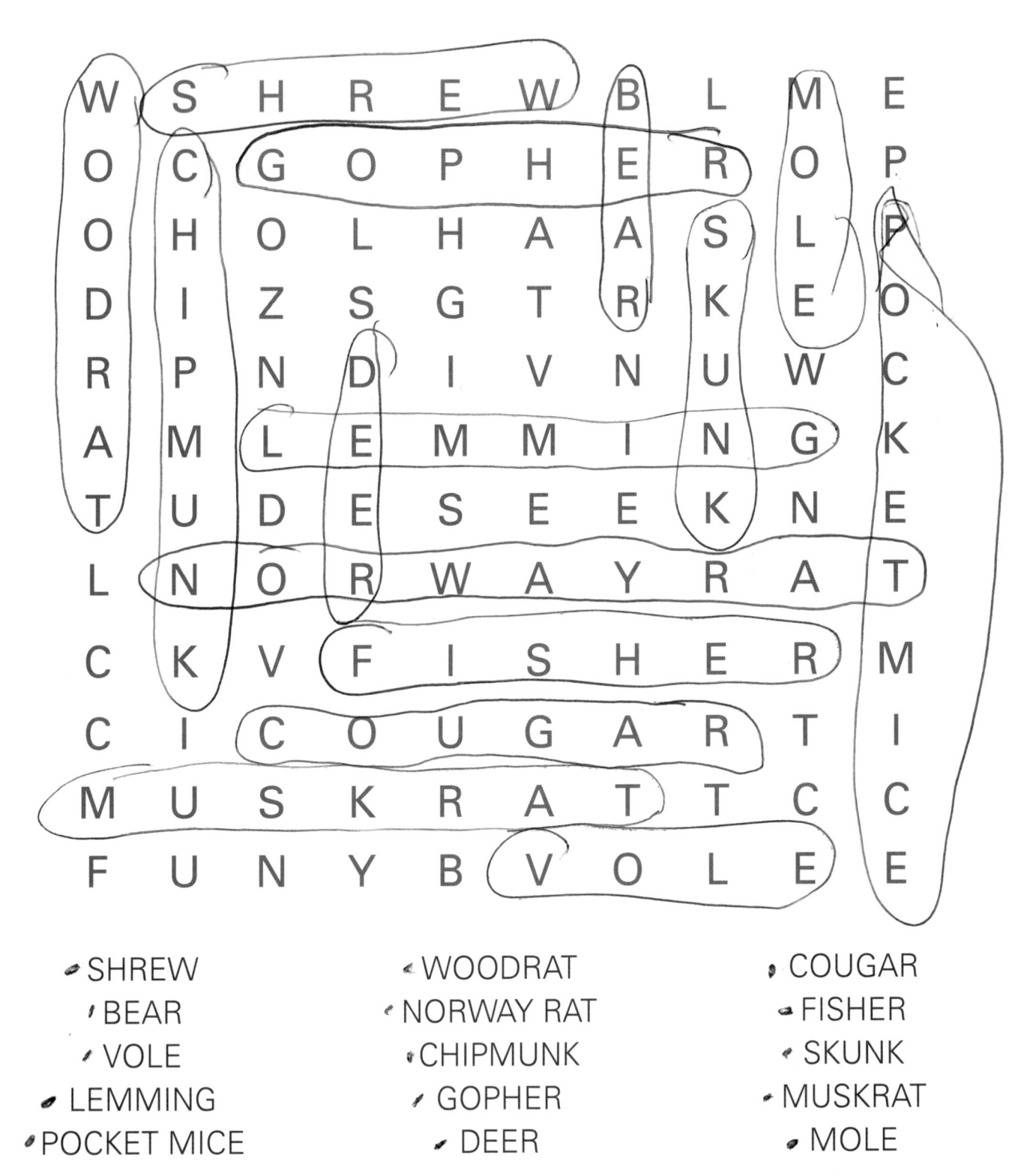

```
W   S   H   R   E   W   B   L   M   E
O   C   G   O   P   H   E   R   O   P
O   H   O   L   H   A   A   S   L   P
D   I   Z   S   G   T   R   K   E   O
R   P   N   D   I   V   N   U   W   C
A   M   L   E   M   M   I   N   G   K
T   U   D   E   S   E   E   K   N   E
L   N   O   R   W   A   Y   R   A   T
C   K   V   F   I   S   H   E   R   M
C   I   C   O   U   G   A   R   T   I
M   U   S   K   R   A   T   T   C   C
F   U   N   Y   B   V   O   L   E   E
```

- SHREW
- BEAR
- VOLE
- LEMMING
- POCKET MICE

- WOODRAT
- NORWAY RAT
- CHIPMUNK
- GOPHER
- DEER

- COUGAR
- FISHER
- SKUNK
- MUSKRAT
- MOLE

**Most of the animals listed are smaller than a coyote.
Bonus: Find the animals larger than a coyote.**

(answers on page 62)

Flying Squirrel Maze

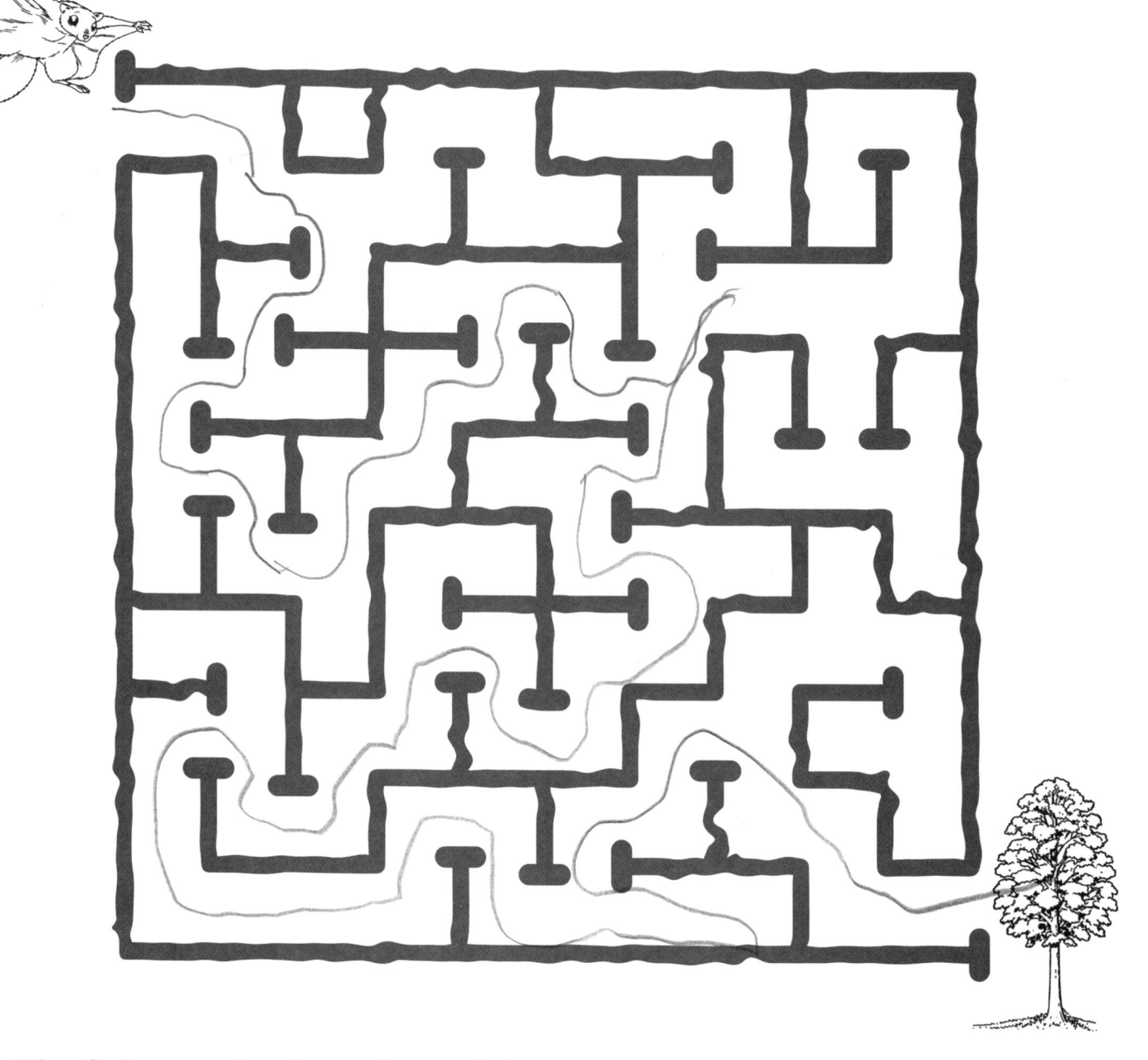

**The flying squirrel needs to glide to the next tree to reach its nest.
Help it find its way there!**

You can sometimes find a flying squirrel's landing spot
in the snow. This landing spot is called a "sitzmark."

(answer on page 62)

Name the Animals

MOOSE

COTTONTAIL RABBIT

BEAVER

BLACK BEAR

WOLF

SKUNK

Can you identify these animals? Who knows, you might even find these tracks in the wild!

 **What's the biggest animal you've ever seen in the wild? The smallest? How many animals have you seen today?**

(answers on page 62)

Groups of Tracks

Can you guess what these animals were doing when they made these groups of tracks? For a clue, finish the matching activity on page 30.

PORCUPINE	**WHITE-TAILED DEER**	**COTTONTAIL RABBIT**
(A) walking slowly	A. sitting still	(A) hopping
B. jumping	(B) skipping	B. walking really slowly
C. sitting still	C. jumping	C. running really fast
D. sprinting	D. running really fast (called galloping)	D. sitting still

Animals can vary their speed just like you, and different speeds/types of walks (gaits) leave different sets of tracks.

(answer on page 62)

11

Southern Flying Squirrel

FRONT TRACK

BACK TRACK

HOPPING

Despite their name, flying squirrels don't actually fly. Instead, they use special skin flaps to glide from tree to tree, and they usually glide 10 to 20 feet. Because they spend a lot of time in trees, their tracks are hard to spot. If you want to try, look in freshly fallen snow.

Flying squirrels are most active at night, and so are the only true flying mammals: bats!

12

Gray Wolf

FRONT TRACK

BACK TRACK

WALKING

Gray wolves were once very common in North America. They became rare due to hunting. Today, wolf populations are growing again, thanks to the work of biologists and other scientists. Because wolves are members of the dog family, wolf tracks look somewhat like those left by domestic dogs.

 Often feared as a predator, gray wolf attacks on people are very rare. There are only a few recorded attacks in history.

What to Bring

One of the great things about animal tracking is that you don't need any equipment to do it! With that said, bringing along a few things certainly doesn't hurt! The following items will make your tracking adventures easier and more productive.

✓ **TAPE MEASURE** (to measure the individual footprints (and the entire track)

✓ **MAGNIFYING GLASS**

✓ **JOURNAL AND PEN/PENCIL**

✓ **BINOCULARS** (for spotting animals in the distance)

✓ **CAMERA OR SMARTPHONE**

✓ **WATER**

✓ **BUG SPRAY**

✓ **HAT**

✓ **FIELD GUIDE**

✓ **MATERIALS FOR MAKING A CAST OF A TRACK** (see page 59)

Virginia Opossum

FRONT TRACK

BACK TRACK

WALKING

Opossums are related to kangaroos: both are marsupials (*mar-SOUP-eee-uls*). Young opossums are carried in a "pouch" on their mother's stomach for two months. Identifying a clear opossum track is easy; its back track looks a lot like a small human handprint.

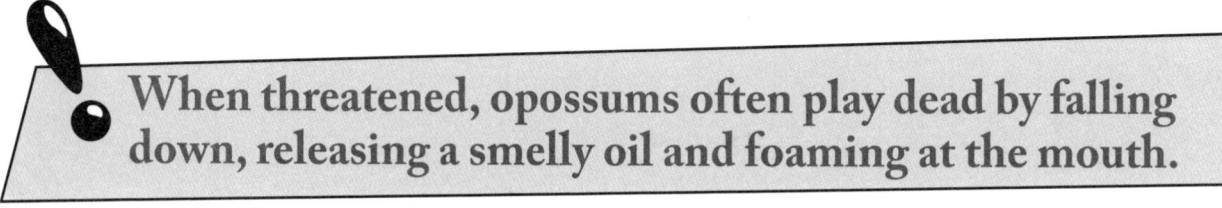

When threatened, opossums often play dead by falling down, releasing a smelly oil and foaming at the mouth.

White-tailed Deer

FRONT TRACK

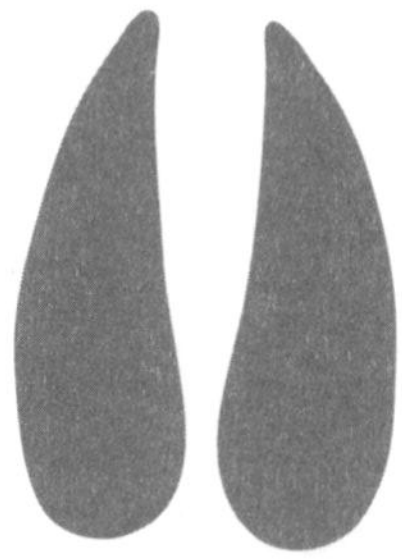

BACK TRACK

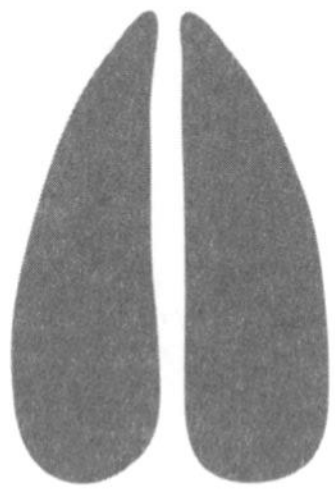

WALKING

White-tailed deer are one of the most common and widespread animals in the country, and they can be found everywhere from country roads and farm fields to city parks. You might even see them in your back yard! One great place to look for their heart-shaped tracks is in farm fields.

Deer need minerals to grow antlers each year; that's why people put blocks of "deer minerals" in their yards to help deer.

Northern Raccoon

FRONT TRACK

BACK TRACK

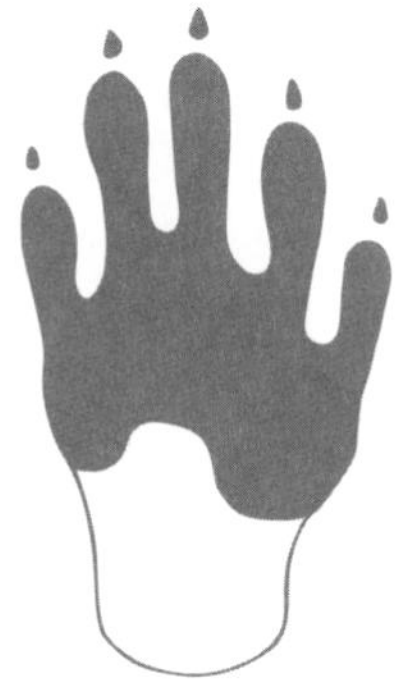

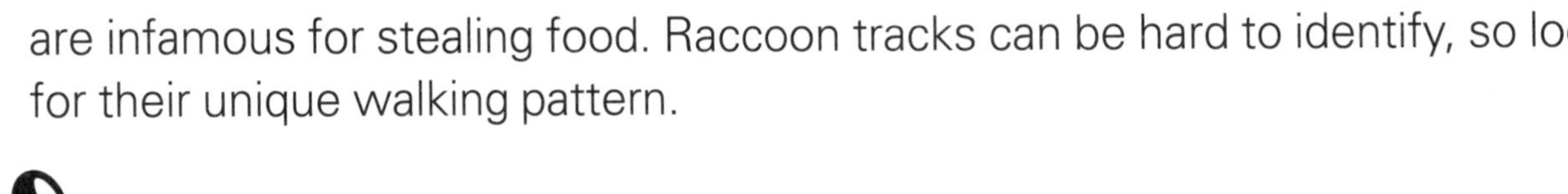

WALKING

A common sight at bird feeders, the northern raccoon is often thought of as a thief. That makes sense; raccoons look like they are wearing a mask, and they are infamous for stealing food. Raccoon tracks can be hard to identify, so look for their unique walking pattern.

> Raccoons are known for "washing" their food before eating, but they aren't actually washing it. Instead, they are probably using their very sensitive hands to feel it.

Fill in the Blanks

```
___ ___ T
___ ___ R ___
___ ___ A ___ ___ ___
___ ___ ___ C ___ ___ ___ ___ ___
___ ___ ___ K ___ ___ ___
___ ___ ___ ___ I ___
___ ___ N ___
___ ___ ___ G ___ ___
```

1. These pets are often allowed outside, so you might find their tracks!

2. This relative of the cottontail rabbit wears "snowshoes" so it can walk on top of snow in the winter.

3. It uses its sharp front teeth to chop down trees, and it is famous for its lodges.

4. This animal's sharp quills protect it from most predators.

5. This large rodent lives mostly in the water and is known for its "musky" smell.

6. These very small mammals are often said to jump off cliffs, but that's not actually true.

7. A large member of the cat family, this animal is found in the northern part of the country.

8. Hunters once used dachshunds, a special type of dog, to hunt this animal.

18   (answers on page 62)

Porcupine

FRONT TRACK

BACK TRACK

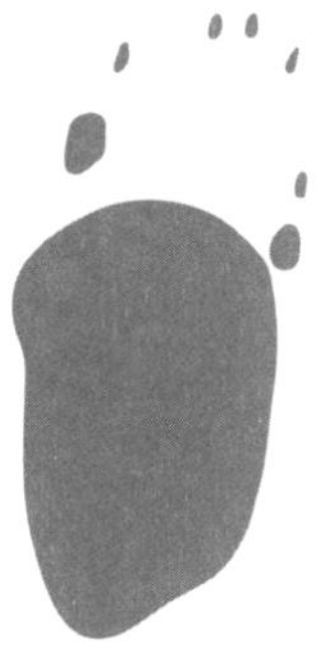

WALKING

A funny-looking creature, the porcupine is covered in long, sharp quills. From a distance, these quills look soft, but they are very sharp. Because they are protected by their quills, porcupines generally walk along slowly, as they don't usually need to run away from predators.

 **Sometimes, porcupines accidentally get hurt by their own quills. Thankfully, porcupine quills are covered in special medicines (antibiotics) that prevent infection.**

North American Beaver

FRONT TRACK

BACK TRACK

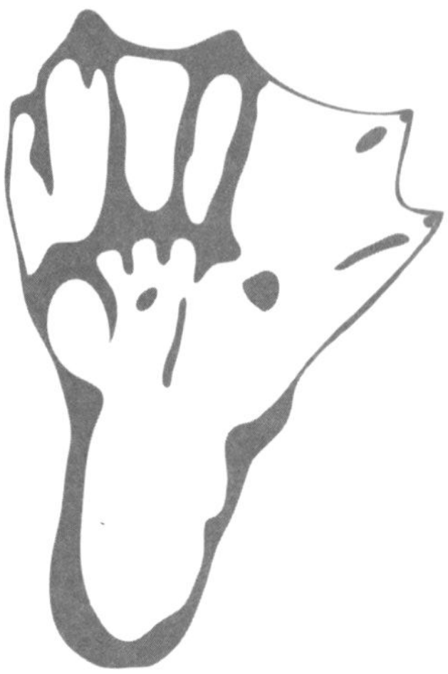

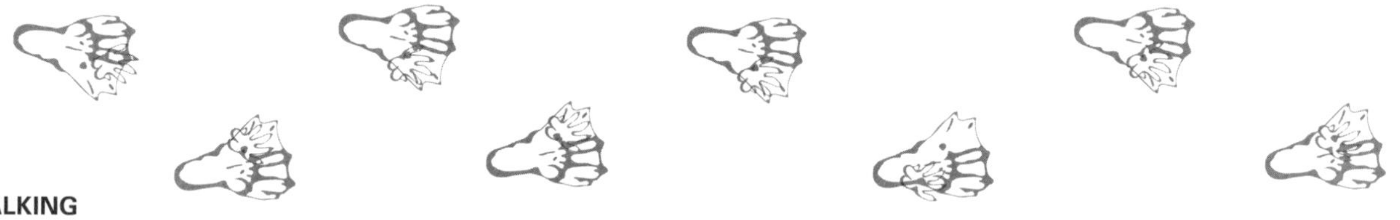

WALKING

Beavers use sticks and mud to build their houses, which are called lodges. Beavers also build dams, which block the flow of water, creating deep pools that protect beavers from predators and make it easier for beavers to find food. A beaver's rear tracks are huge, twice the size of its front tracks.

Some beaver dams are huge. One beaver dam in Canada can be seen from space! It's over 40 years old, and generations of beavers have worked on it.

Woodrat

FRONT TRACK

BACK TRACK

WALKING

Woodrats are famous for building large, complicated dens. They often find everyday objects—especially shiny ones—and incorporate them into their nests. Woodrat tracks look a bit like the tracks of other rodents, but their toe pads are more rounded than in other mice or rats.

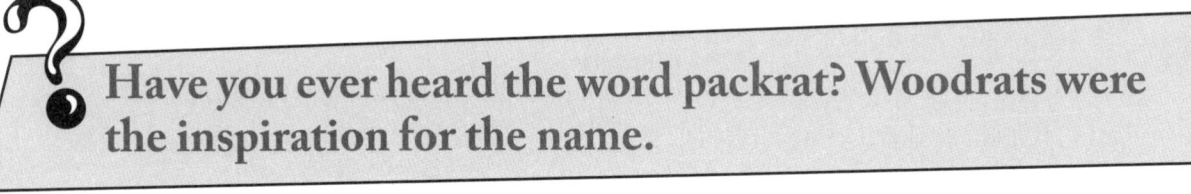

Have you ever heard the word packrat? Woodrats were the inspiration for the name.

House Mouse

FRONT TRACK

BACK TRACK

WALKING

The house mouse usually lives near people, and they build nests in all sorts of places, including cupboards and basements, and even under the hoods of cars. Because they often live indoors, mouse tracks can be hard to find. But its scat (poop) is easy to spot and is often the first sign that mice are present.

When people started living in towns, this attracted mice, which then attracted cats. The tamest cats reproduced the most, eventually leading to a new species: the house cat!

Prairie Dog Maze

Prairie dogs live in "towns," large networks of tunnels that feature many rooms. Help the prairie dog find its way out of the prairie dog town!

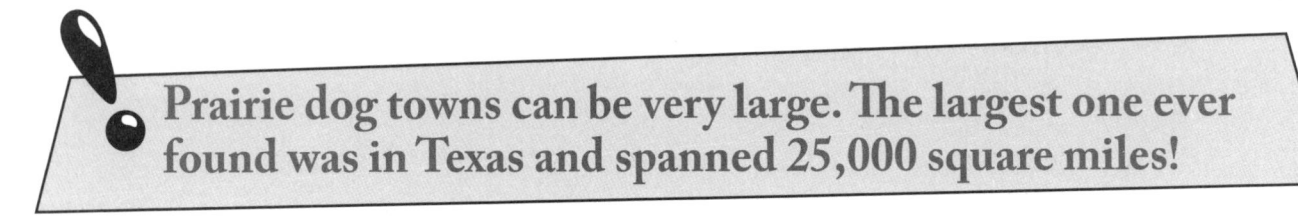

Prairie dog towns can be very large. The largest one ever found was in Texas and spanned 25,000 square miles!

(answer on page 62)

Red Fox

FRONT TRACK

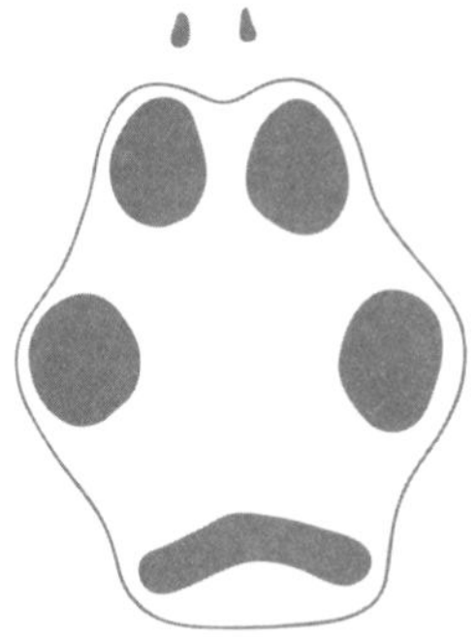

BACK TRACK

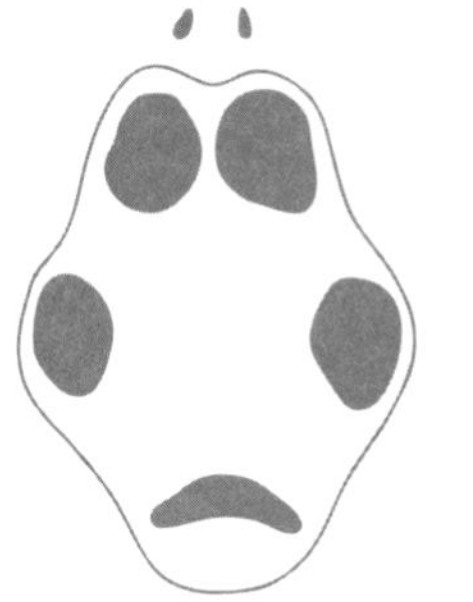

TROTTING

Foxes are famous for being smart and curious. Foxes don't just live in the woods, they also live close to people—in city parks, suburbs, even in back-yards—so you might be surprised where their dog-like tracks turn up.

So what *does* the fox say? Like dogs, foxes bark, though their bark sounds more like a scream than a "bowwow."

House Cat

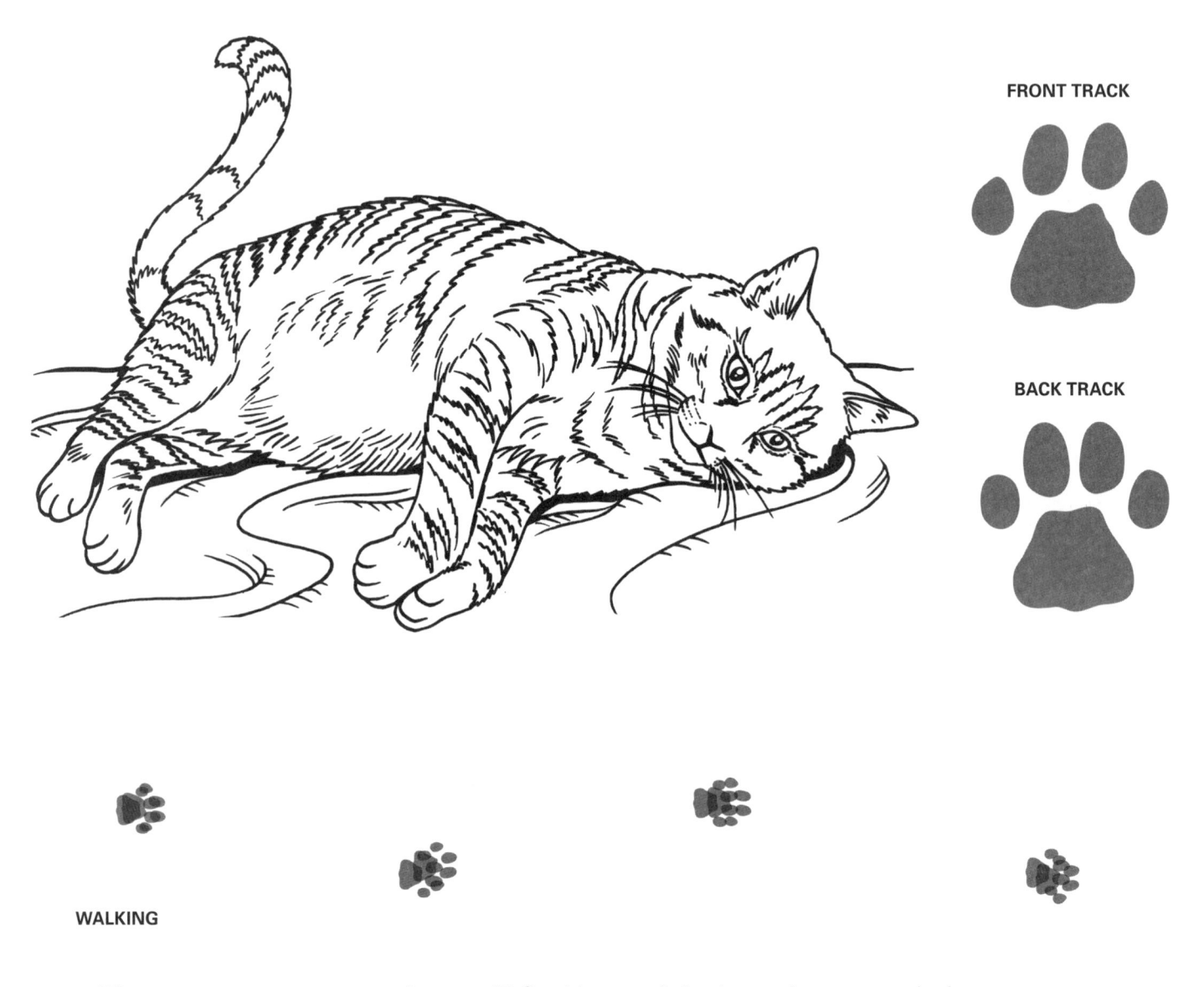

FRONT TRACK

BACK TRACK

WALKING

The most common tracks you'll find just might have been made by your pet kitty. Many people let their pet cats outside, where cats often hunt birds and other animals. Stray cats also leave lots of tracks behind. So take a look and see if you can find some cat tracks in your neighborhood.

Want to see an animal track up close? Take a look at your pet cat's foot; just watch out for its claws!

Crack the Code!

Use the code below to identify 10 animals.

1	2	3	4	5	6	7	8	9	10	11	12	13	14	15	16	17	18	19	20	21	22	23	24	25	26
A	B	C	D	E	F	G	H	I	J	K	L	M	N	O	P	Q	R	S	T	U	V	W	X	Y	Z

1. Because of overbreeding and released pets, there is a large H _ _ _ _ _ _ _
population in the wild.
8 15 21 19 5   3 1 20

2. The _ _ _ _ _ _ _ _ _ _ _ lives underground in a "town" that has many
16 18 1 9 18 9 5 4 15 7
chambers and rooms.

3. Related to the wolf and your pet dog, the _ _ _ _ _ _ is famous for its howl.
3 15 25 15 20 5

4. Once one of the most common animals on the Great Plains, wild populations of
the _ _ _ _ _ are very rare today.
2 9 19 15 1

5. The _ _ _ _ _ _ is famous for its paddle-shaped tail and its sharp front teeth.
2 5 1 22 5 18

6. The _ _ _ _ _ _ _ _ _ _ _ _ is an unwelcome guest in kitchens, cupboards
8 15 21 19 5 13 15 21 19 5
and pantries.

7. The largest species of deer, the _ _ _ _ _ can weigh more than 1500 pounds.
13 15 15 19 5

8. The _ _ _ _ _ might look cute, but get too close and you might smell its "perfume."
19 11 21 14 11

9. It may look slow, but the _ _ _ _ _ _ _ _ _ can run over 35 miles per hour.
2 12 1 3 11 2 5 1 18

10. The _ _ _ _ _ _ is also known as the puma or the mountain lion.
3 15 21 7 1 18

Decipher this bonus code for an animal that doesn't leave a track: 6 9 19 8.

(answers on page 62)

Elk

FRONT TRACK

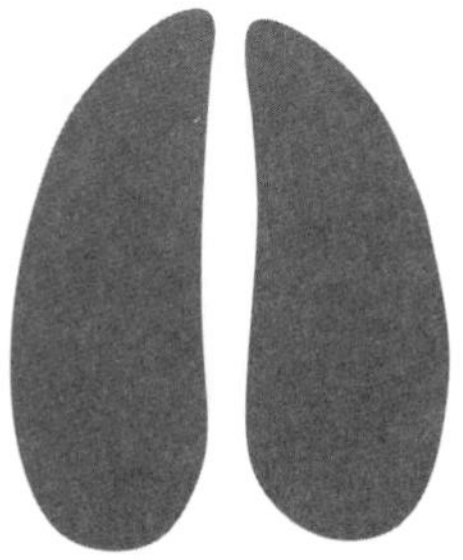

BACK TRACK

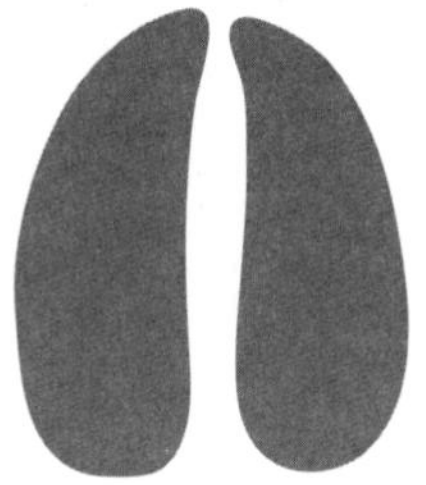

WALKING

Like the moose, elk are members of the deer family and male elk have large antlers. Once found all over North America, today elk are only found in the western portion of the country. Like all deer tracks, elk tracks are heart shaped.

Male elk sometimes use their antlers to fight each other to determine who can reproduce with females.

Help the Beaver Reach Its Lodge!

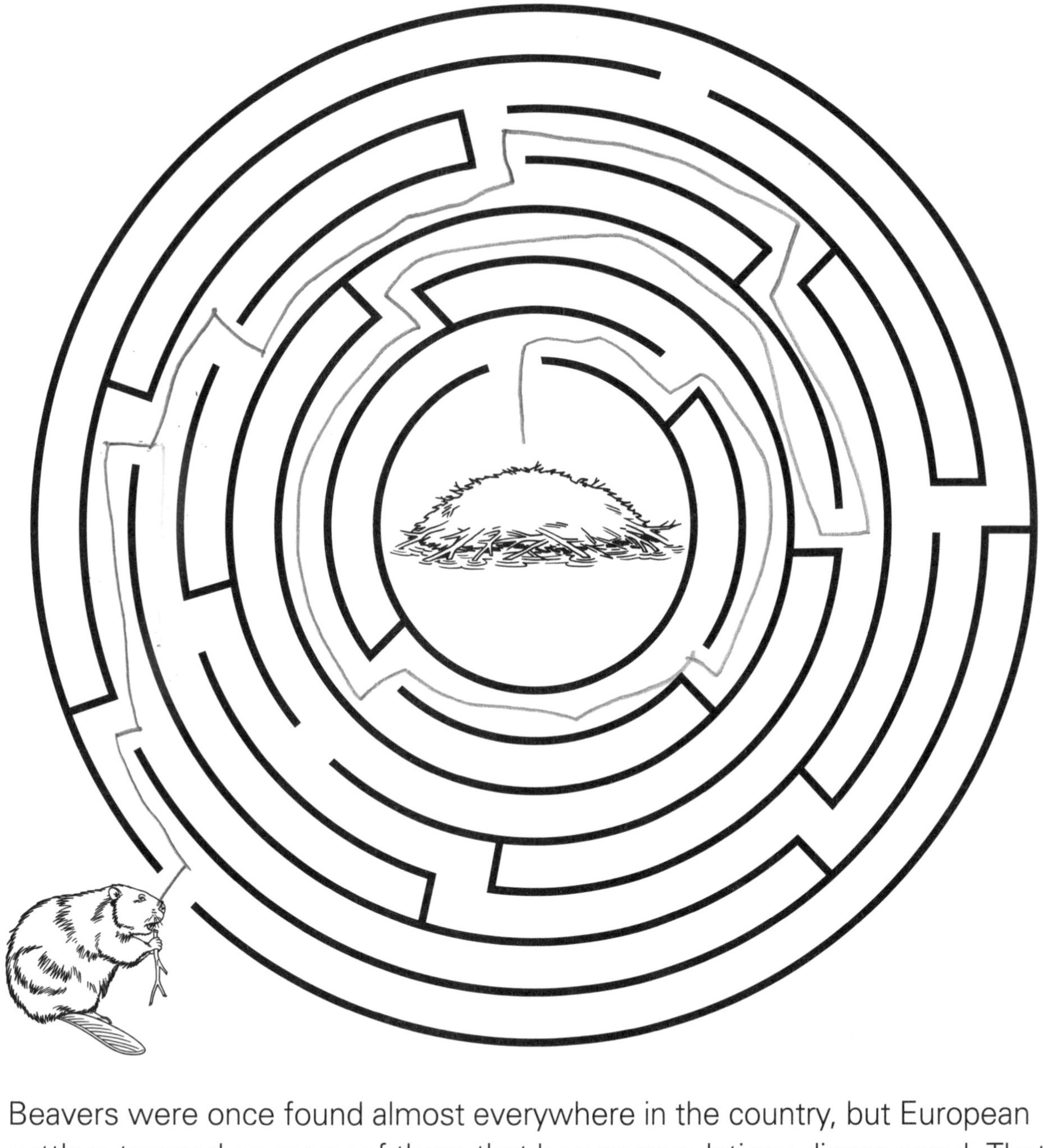

Beavers were once found almost everywhere in the country, but European settlers trapped so many of them that beaver populations disappeared. That's changing today. In New York City, beavers hadn't been spotted for 200 years; that changed in 2007, when a beaver was spotted in the Bronx River.

Beaver populations were almost wiped out because of the fur trade. What was beaver skin used for? Fancy hats.

(answers on page 63)

Woodchuck

FRONT TRACK

BACK TRACK

WALKING

Also called a groundhog, the woodchuck mostly lives underground. Despite the famous tongue-twister, woodchucks don't chuck or throw wood. The name probably come from the Algonquian Indian word *wuchak*. Woodchuck tracks show their sharp claws, which they use to dig burrows.

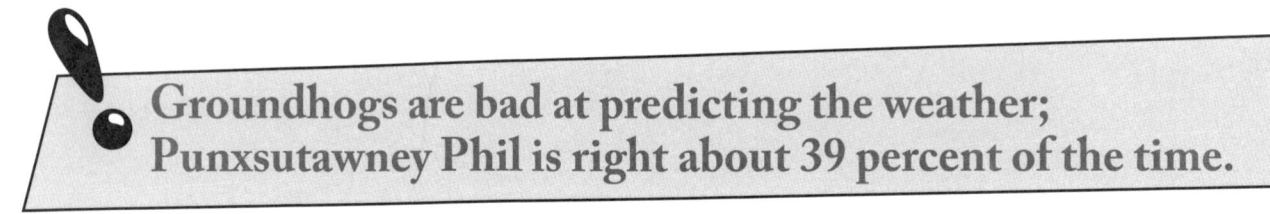

Groundhogs are bad at predicting the weather; Punxsutawney Phil is right about 39 percent of the time.

Gaits

COTTONTAIL RABBIT

PORCUPINE

GRAY WOLF

TROT

BOUND

WALK

The pattern an animal's feet makes as it moves is called a gait. There are many kinds of gaits. **Walking** is a type of gait, and so is **galloping** (running). A **trot** is faster than a walk but slower than a run. An animal that **bounds** (hops) uses its limbs to leap forward. Each type of gait leaves a set of footprints that looks different.

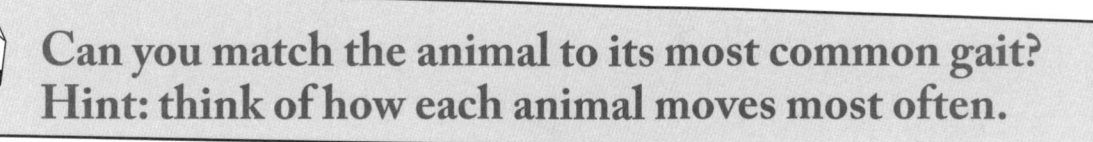

Can you match the animal to its most common gait? Hint: think of how each animal moves most often.

(answers on page 63)

Looking Closely

HOUSE MOUSE

MOLE

SHREWS

NORWAY RAT

HARVEST MICE

When you're animal tracking, it's important to look closely at tracks, and this is especially true if you're tracking smaller animals. The tracks above all belong to small mammals that prefer to avoid being found. But you still might find their tracks. If you do, look closely and see if you can identify them!

> **Small animals often leave tracks that are hard to see, so bring a magnifying glass to get a closer look.**

Cottontail Rabbit

FRONT TRACK

BACK TRACK

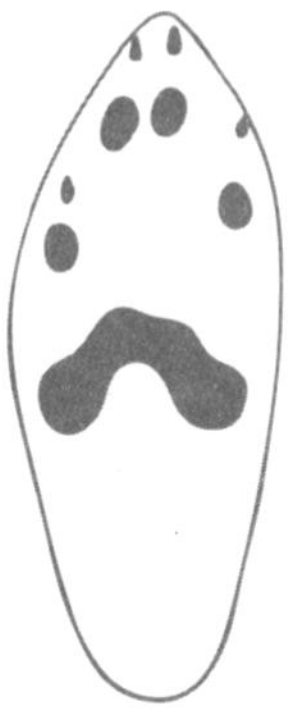

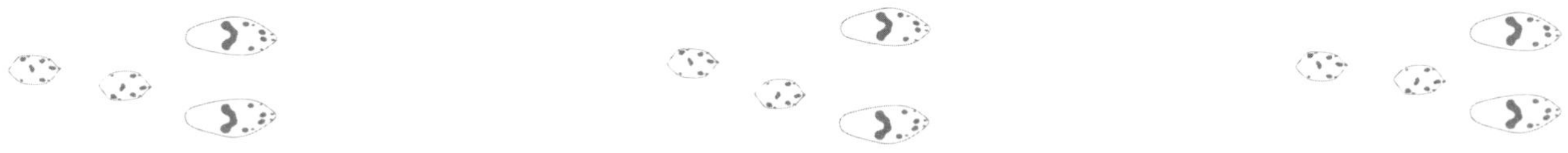

BOUNDING

Famous for its fluffy tail, the cottontail rabbit is a common sight in many areas, including backyards. Cottontails almost always bound (hop) and this leaves a distinct pattern that makes it easy to identify their tracks.

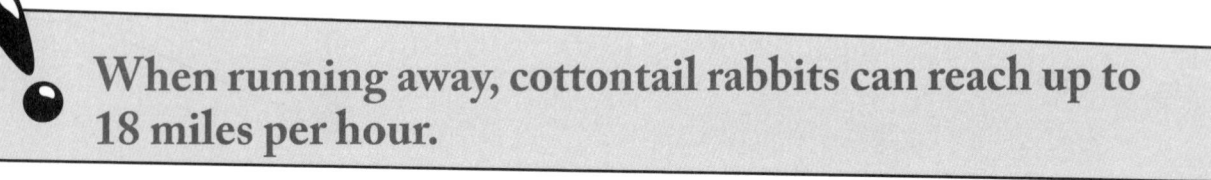

When running away, cottontail rabbits can reach up to 18 miles per hour.

Snowshoe Hare

FRONT TRACK

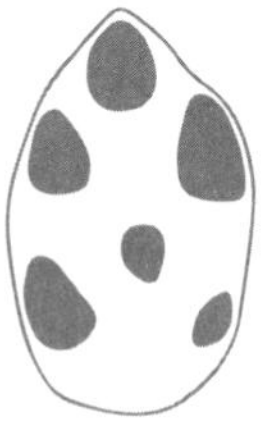

BACK TRACK

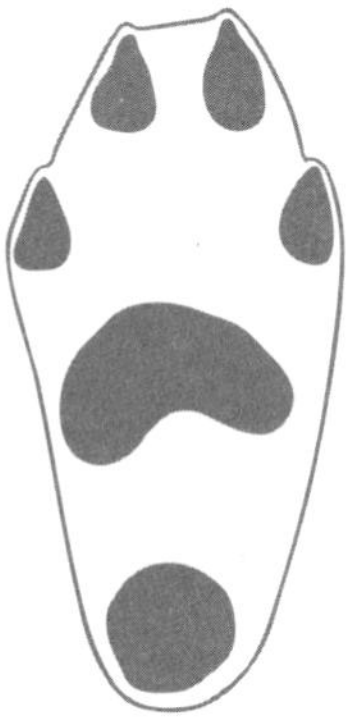

BOUNDING

Found in the northern part of the U.S., snowshoe hares are well adapted for winter. They are named for their large, furry feet that help them walk on top of snow. Their rear feet are much larger than their front ones, and this is easy to see in their tracks.

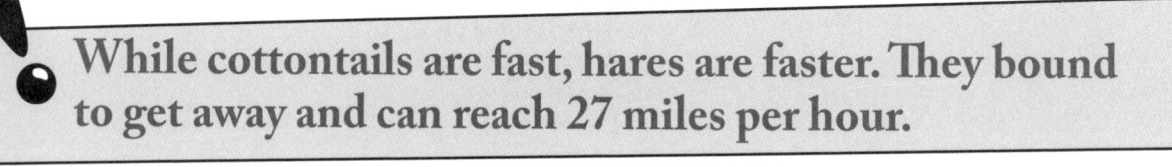

While cottontails are fast, hares are faster. They bound to get away and can reach 27 miles per hour.

Animal Names Crossword

Across

1. This rodent sometimes carries extra food in its cheeks

5. It can chop down huge trees with its teeth

7. These black-and-white "thieves" are often seen near trash bins

9. Its armor helps protect it from predators

Down

2. A blind animal that lives underground

3. It uses its large, furry feet to stay on top of the snow

4. A structure that beavers build to make the water deeper

5. At several hundred pounds, it looks slow, but it can run 35 miles per hour

6. It can't really predict the weather

8. Animal droppings that can help you identify a track

Fill the crossword above to learn about animals and tracking!

(answers on page 63)

Striped Skunk

FRONT TRACK

BACK TRACK

WALKING

You may not have seen a skunk, but you've probably smelled one. Skunks are well known for their stinky spray, which they use to defend themselves against predators. Because of their well-advertised defense, skunks aren't usually in much of a hurry; they usually walk along, and this is often seen in their tracks.

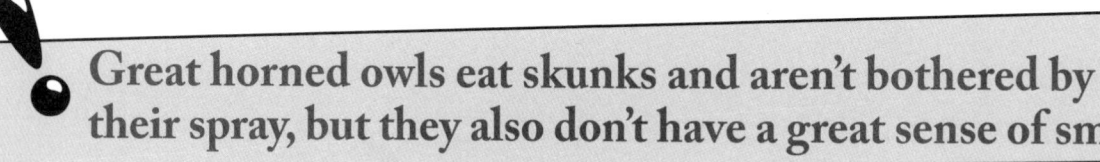

Great horned owls eat skunks and aren't bothered by their spray, but they also don't have a great sense of smell.

Black-tailed Prairie Dog

FRONT TRACK

BACK TRACK

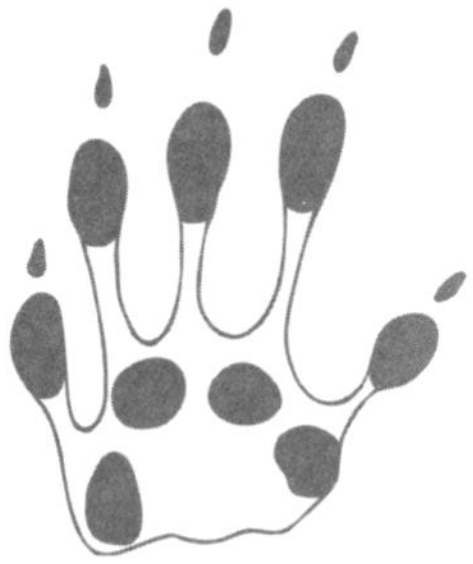

WALKING

Some animals prefer to be alone. Not prairie dogs. They live in large underground "towns" that are divided into neighborhoods called wards. Each ward is home to a family of prairie dogs. Prairie dogs even post lookouts to watch for predators. You can find many tracks near a prairie dog burrow.

Prairie dogs got their name because settlers thought prairie dog chirps sounded like a dog's bark.

How Many Mammals?

Mammals are often hard to find, and that is no accident. Mammals like staying hidden because it helps keep them safe from predators. That's one reason that many mammals have brown or gray fur; it helps them blend in!

How many mammals can you find in the picture above? What animal sticks out the most?

(answers on page 63)

Coyote

FRONT TRACK

BACK TRACK

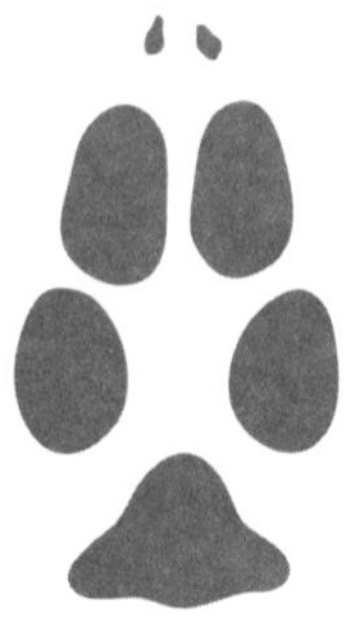

WALKING

Related to dogs and wolves, coyotes can be found throughout North America, even in big cities. Even though they're predators, coyotes are shy and avoid people. Coyote tracks can be hard to tell apart from dog tracks; if you see one in your area, don't worry, it's probably Fido.

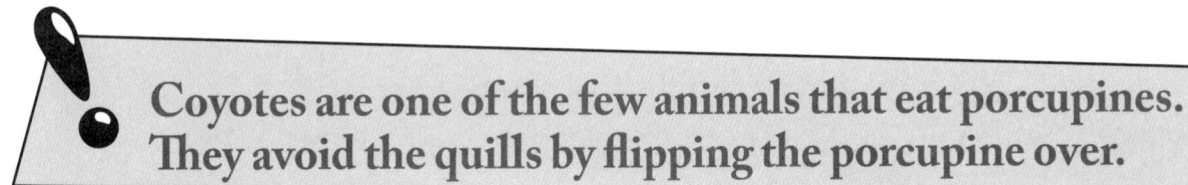

Coyotes are one of the few animals that eat porcupines. They avoid the quills by flipping the porcupine over.

Match the Tracks

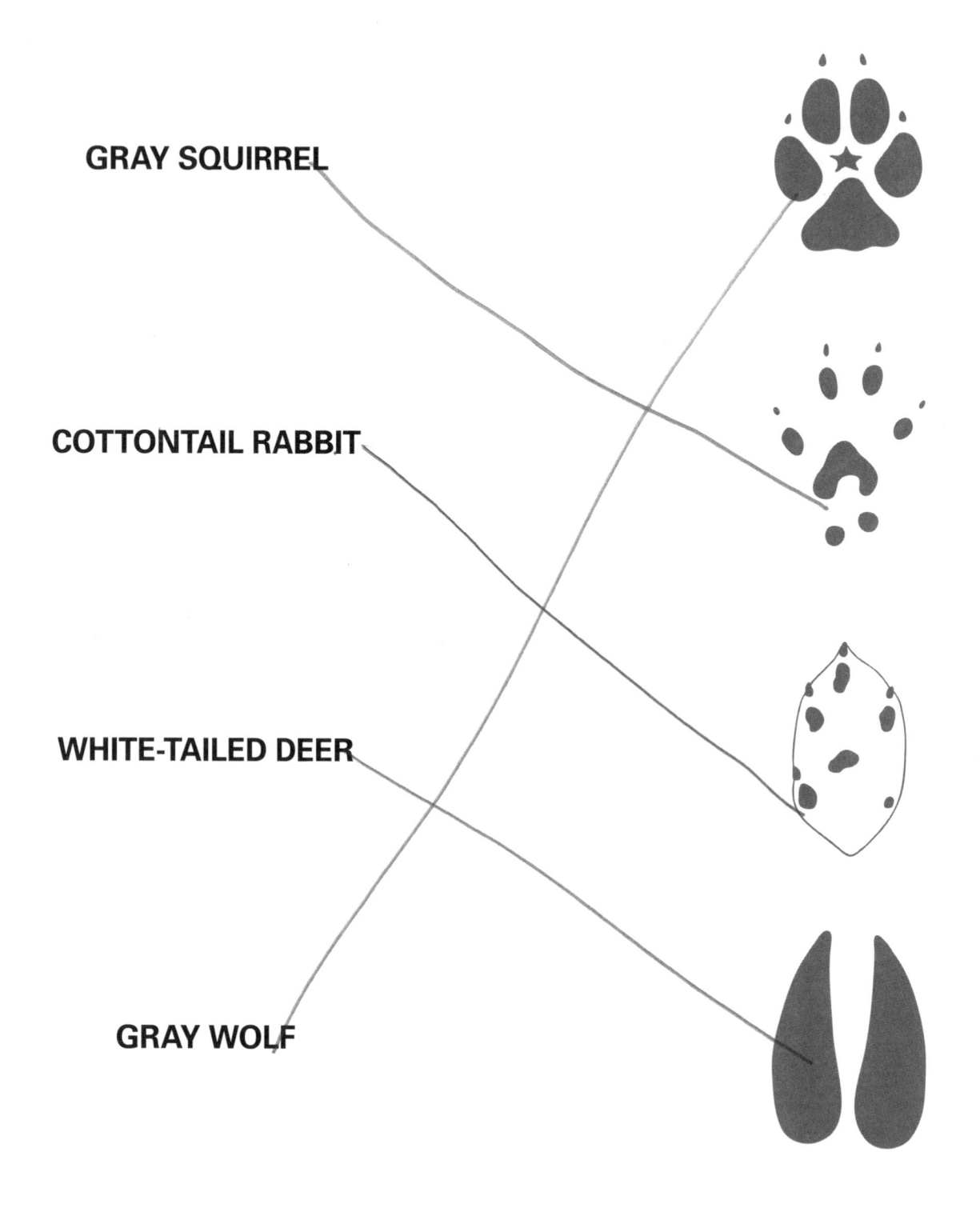

GRAY SQUIRREL

COTTONTAIL RABBIT

WHITE-TAILED DEER

GRAY WOLF

Which animal made the track above?
Note: In real life, these tracks aren't all the same size.

(answers on page 63)

Weasel

FRONT TRACK

BACK TRACK

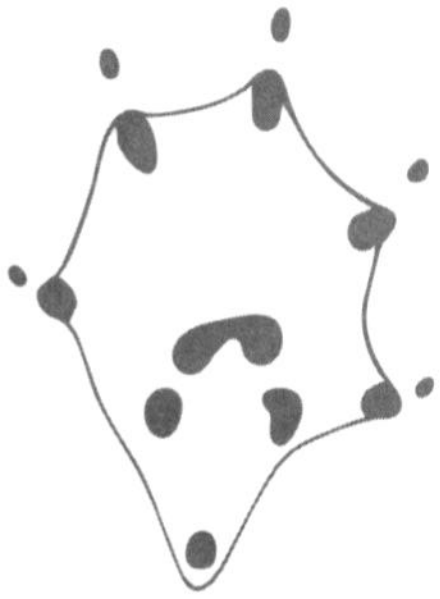

LOPING

Weasels are small, skinny animals and very good hunters despite their small size. There are several different species of weasels in the U.S., and they can be found in much of the country. Weasels are very curious, so their trails often don't head in a straight line, but instead have many turns and detours.

The fur of the least weasel glows under ultraviolet light!

Bobcat

FRONT TRACK

BACK TRACK

BOUNDING

Bobcats are small wildcats found in a number of different environments, including forests, mountainous regions, and even near deserts. Bobcats eat small mammals and birds. Bobcats are rare in suburban areas and in cities. If you've found a track that looks like a bobcat's, it's probably a house cat's.

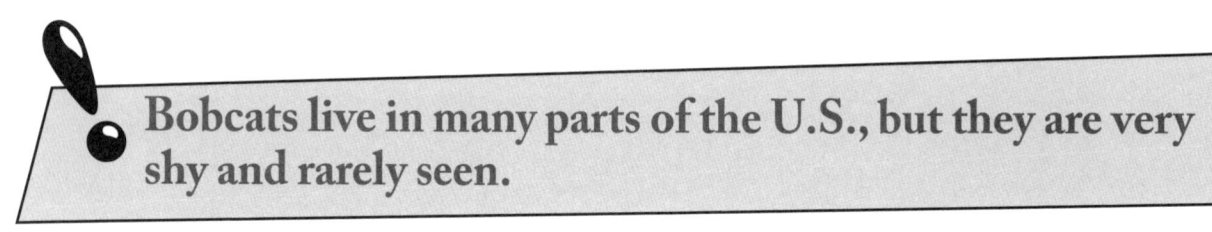

Bobcats live in many parts of the U.S., but they are very shy and rarely seen.

Bird Tracks

AMERICAN CROW

ROCK PIGEON

Birds leave tracks behind, too! While bird tracks are small, they are easy to spot, thanks to their unique shape, which is often fork-like. Bird tracks get this shape from their toe structure (which varies by species). The tracks above are from two pretty common species in the U.S.

Many field guides don't cover bird tracks. For one that does, see page 61.

Red Squirrel

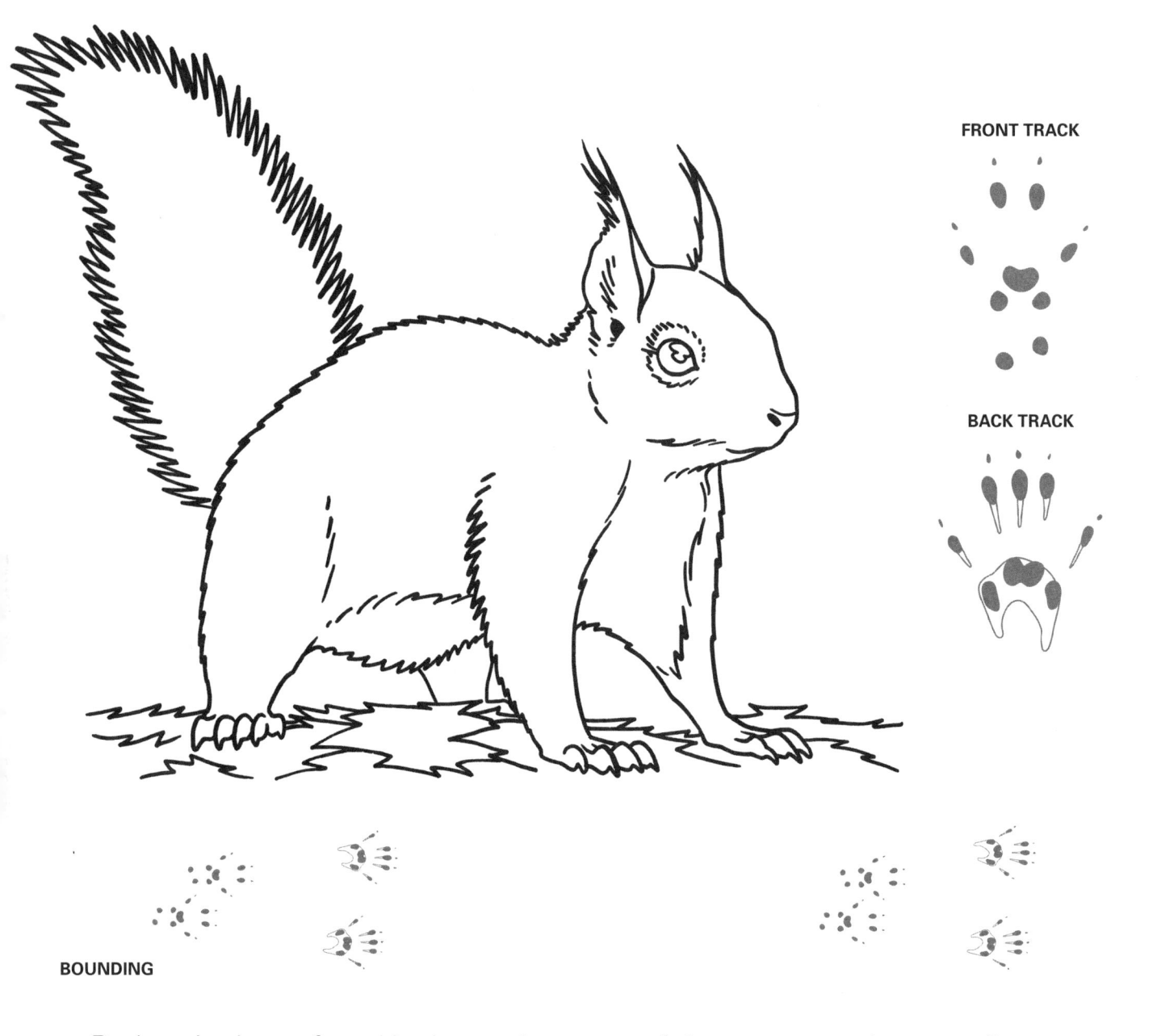

FRONT TRACK

BACK TRACK

BOUNDING

Red squirrels are found in the northern part of the country and are smaller than gray squirrels. Red squirrel tracks look like those of other squirrels, but it's not that hard to know if a red squirrel is in the area: they make a lot more noise! Red squirrels will even whistle or chirp at people nearby.

To prepare for winter, red squirrels store food in advance in small piles called "middens."

Track Shapes

NORTHERN RACCOON

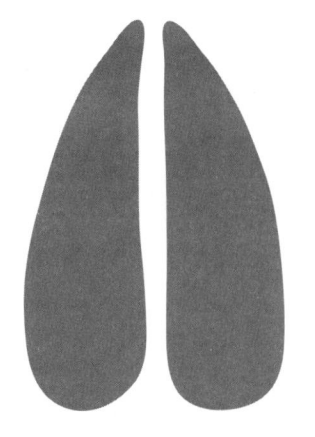

WHITE-TAILED DEER

EASTERN COTTONTAIL

GRAY WOLF

Tracks come in all sorts of shapes and sizes. Can you find the following four shapes in the animal tracks above? Look for a hand-shaped track, a heart-shaped one, an oval track, and the track with a star at the center.

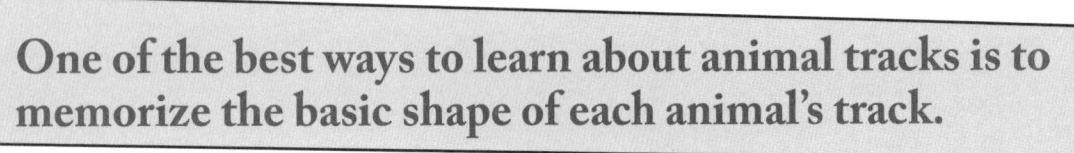

One of the best ways to learn about animal tracks is to memorize the basic shape of each animal's track.

44

Canada Lynx

FRONT TRACK

BACK TRACK

WALKING

Scattered across the northern portions of the U.S., the Canada Lynx looks a bit like a bobcat, but it has longer ear fur, a long, furry "beard" and longer legs than a bobcat. Canada Lynx also have large feet that serve as "snowshoes" and let them walk on top of the snow.

Some animals have a favorite food: Lynx prefer eating snowshoe hares.

Cougar

FRONT TRACK

BACK TRACK

WALKING

The cougar is the second-largest cat in North America (after the jaguar), and the largest regularly spotted in the U.S. Cougar tracks also often don't show claws; that's because cougars have retractable claws, just like your pet cat!

Cougars are found in the western part of the country, but lone cougars have been spotted as far as the East Coast!

Moose

FRONT TRACK

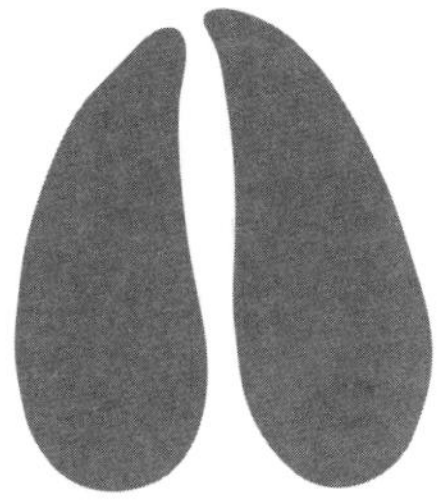

BACK TRACK

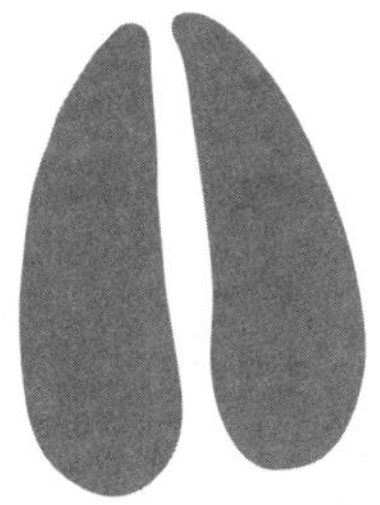

WALKING

A moose stomach has four parts, and in order to eat food, moose have to chew their food twice! This helps their stomach break down the plants they eat. It also leads to a lot of gas, so stay upwind of a moose! Oddly, moose lack the ability to sweat, so they are very sensitive to temperature changes.

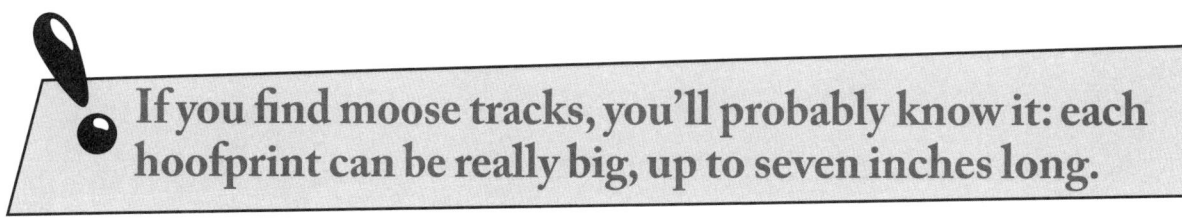

If you find moose tracks, you'll probably know it: each hoofprint can be really big, up to seven inches long.

Solve the Riddles!

I am awake at noon or night,
and I run beneath the forest leaves,
but I have no fright.
I burble and babble, but I speak no words.
Homeless and always on the move,
I am myself home to fish and birds.
What am I?

I have a first name that you know,
but not a last one.
I'm related to the furry friends you tease
with a string or a laser-pointer for fun.
Who am I?

I live in a town, but it has no streets or cars.
I'm a dog but no one's pet.
When there is danger, I stand up on my
back legs to see far.
Do you have an idea who I am yet?

(answers on page 63)

Bison

WALKING

Huge herds of bison were once found all over the country, but they were hunted almost to extinction. Today, a few bison populations still exist; the largest is found at Yellowstone National Park, where you can see 4,600 bison. Bison tracks look a lot like those of their close relative, the cow.

Adult bison can be up to 2000 pounds, almost as much as a small car.

Chipmunk

FRONT TRACK

BACK TRACK

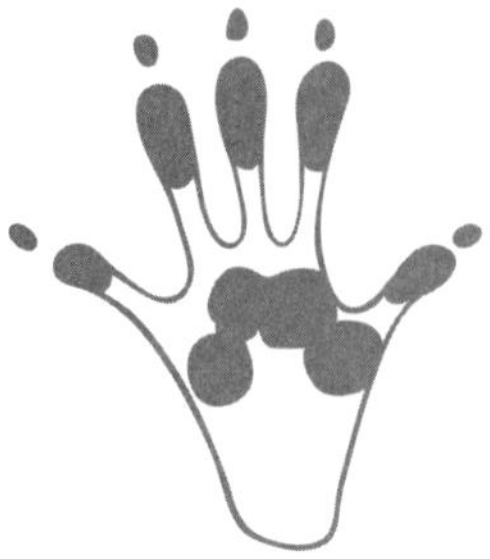

BOUNDING

Small and active, chipmunks are tiny members of the squirrel family. They are found in much of the U.S. They get their name because of the "chip-chip" sound they make when running, and they are easy to spot because of their striped bodies.

Like other squirrels, a chipmunk has four toes on its front feet, but five toes on its back feet!

What Made These Tiny Tracks?

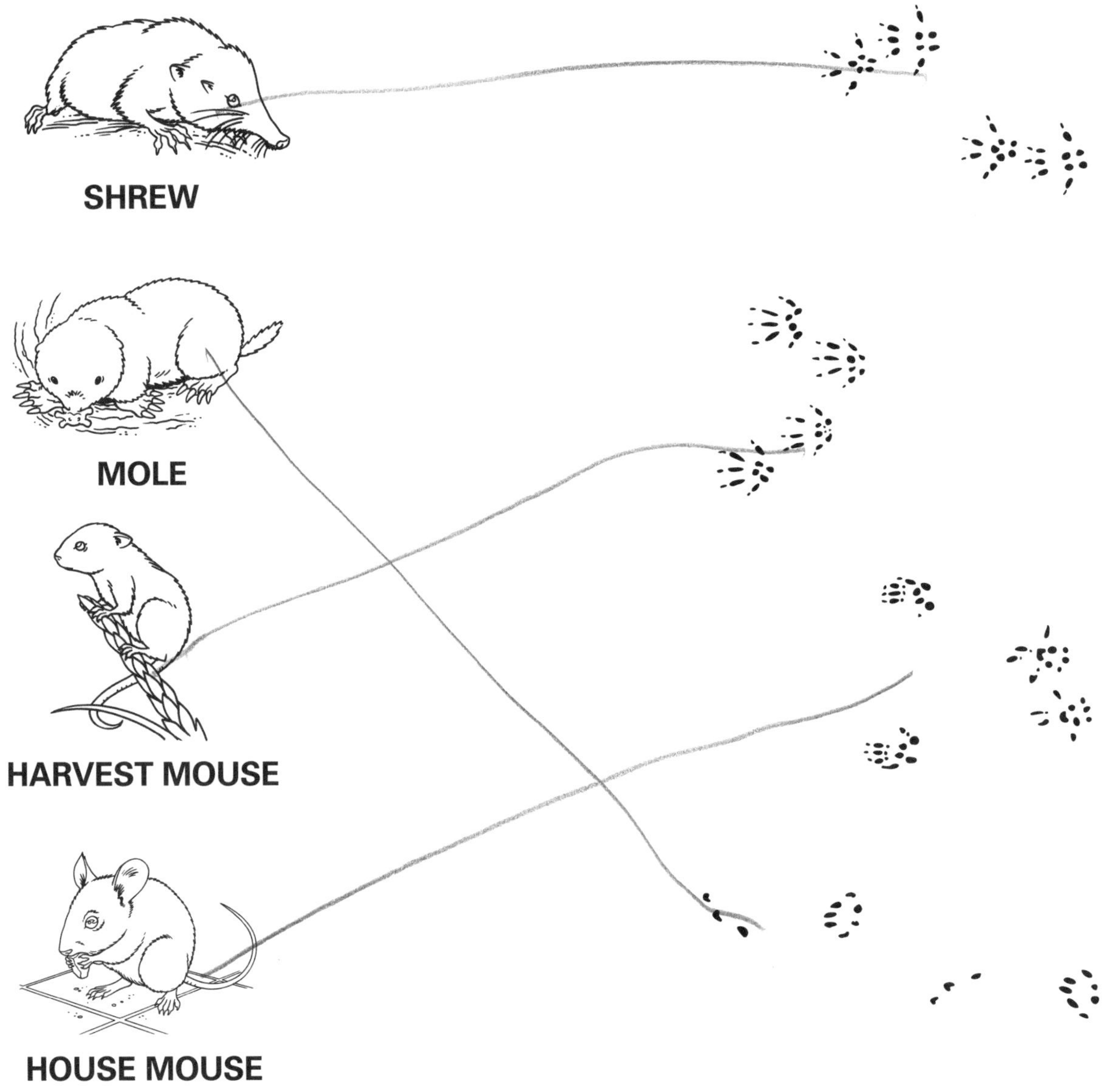

SHREW

MOLE

HARVEST MOUSE

HOUSE MOUSE

Small animals don't just make small tracks, they also make very faint tracks, and their tracks often look similar to one another's. That's why it takes a lot of practice to identify them. Can you guess which animals made these tracks? Hint: Shrews and moles have five toes on both their back and front feet.

If you don't get the answers right, that's OK! Tracking isn't always easy, and practice makes perfect!

(answer on page 64)

Eastern Gray Squirrel

FRONT TRACK

BACK TRACK

WALKING

One of the most common animals in the eastern part of the U.S., gray squirrels are famous for storing food for winter. They hide acorns and other food in the ground. They find many of the acorns, but not all of them. This makes gray squirrels volunteer tree planters!

Stocking up the bird feeder and waiting until a squirrel has visited is a great way to see fresh squirrel tracks!

What Made These Medium-Sized Tracks?

DOMESTIC CAT

SWIFT FOX

SNOWSHOE HARE

BLACK-TAILED PRAIRIE DOG

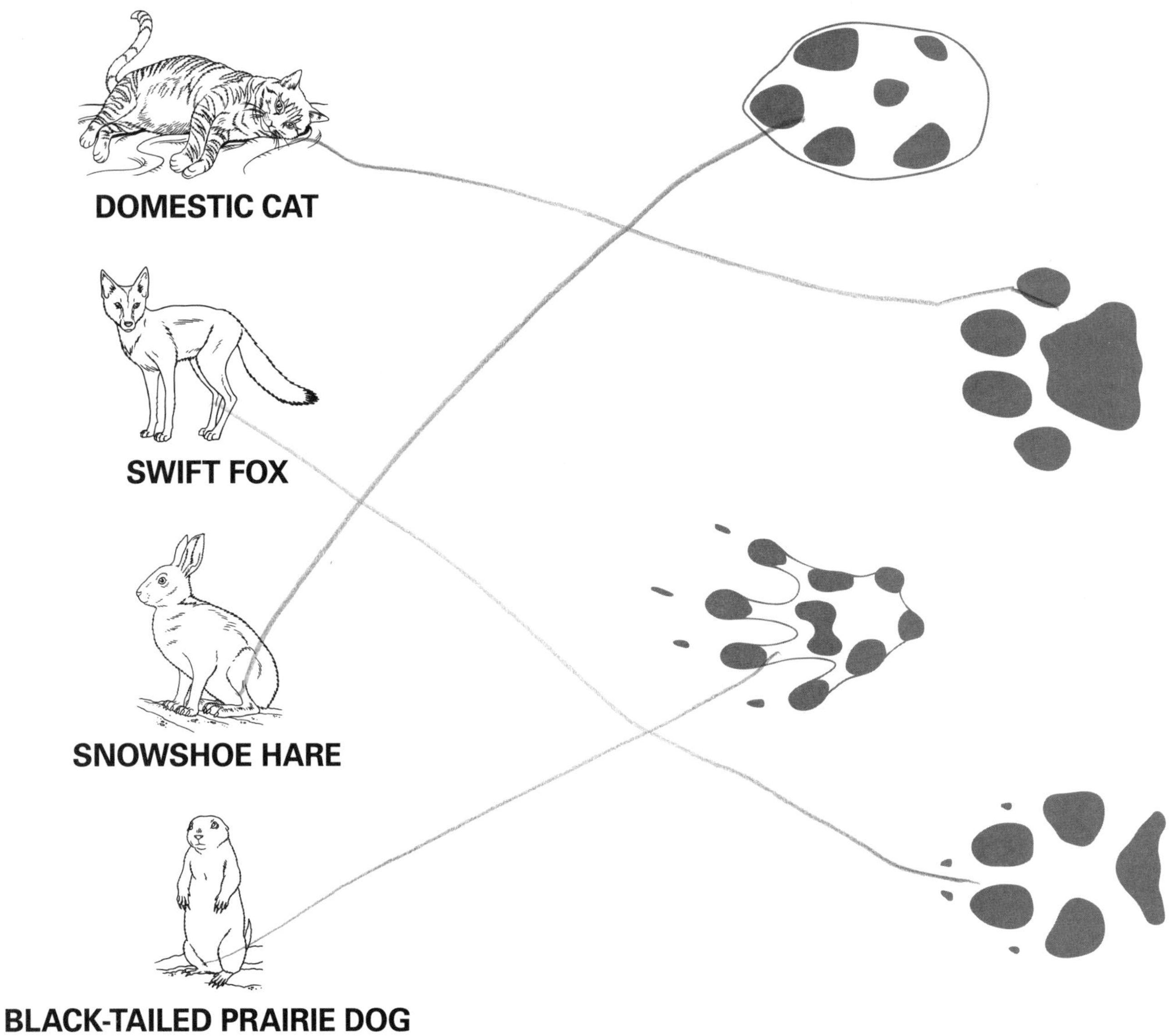

An animal's size doesn't always tell you how large its tracks will be or what they will look like. The animals that made the tracks above are approximately the same size, but their tracks vary in size. Can you guess which animals made these medium-sized tracks?

Look for claws in the tracks above. How many tracks with claws can you see?

(answer on page 64)

Nine-banded Armadillo

FRONT TRACK

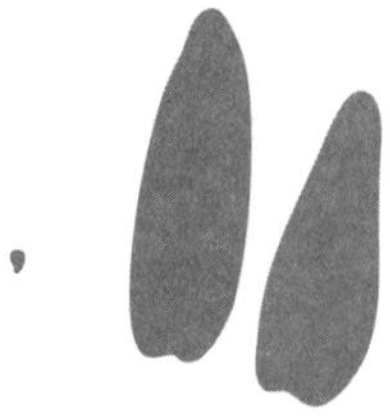

BACK TRACK

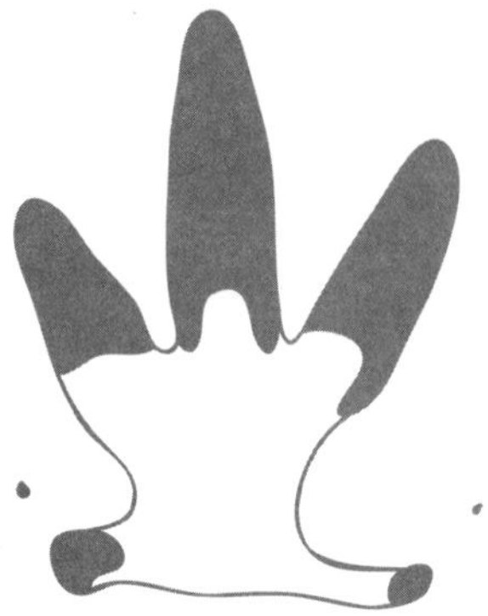

WALKING

Found in the central and southern part of the U.S., the nine-banded armadillo gets its strange name from Spanish explorers who called armadillos "little armored men." The name is a reference to the armadillo's unique armor, which is leathery and is made of keratin pronounced (*carrot-tin*), the same material that makes up your fingernails.

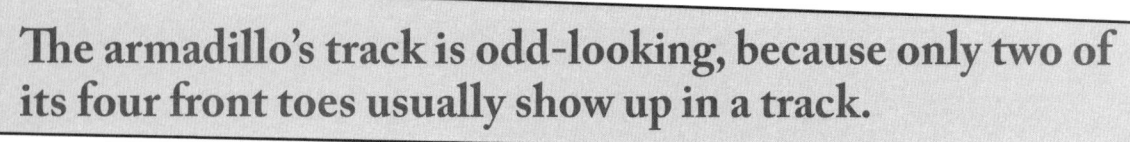

The armadillo's track is odd-looking, because only two of its four front toes usually show up in a track.

What Made These Big Tracks?

1

2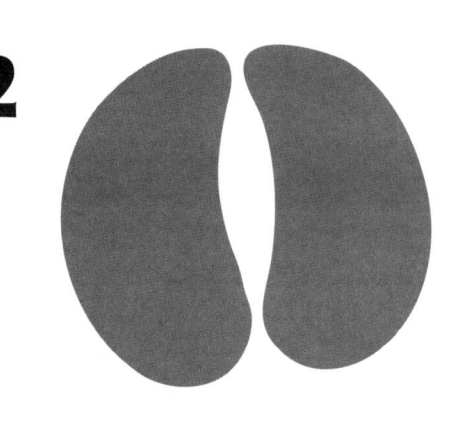

3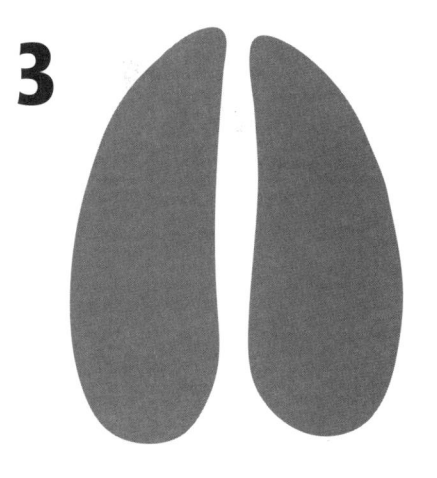

4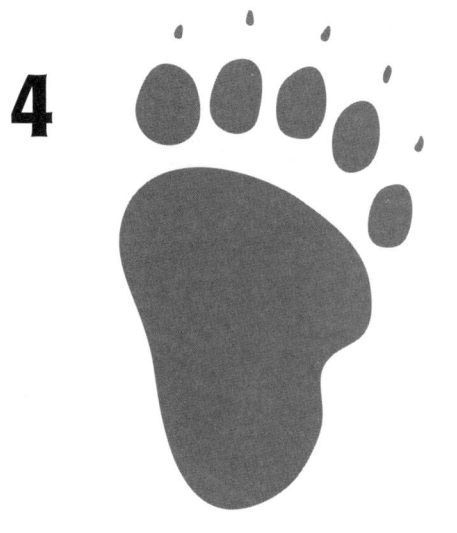

Some animals leave really big tracks! They are so big, it's hard to miss them. Some animal tracks are even bigger than your footprint. What's the largest animal track you've ever found? Write it here: ___elk___.

 **Which animals made these four big tracks? Hint: Here are the four animals: black bear, elk, cougar and bison.**

(answer on page 64)

Bear

FRONT TRACK

BACK TRACK

WALKING

Black bears are found across much of the northern and western part of the country. People are often afraid of black bears, but black bears very rarely attack humans. In fact, they usually eat berries, plants and even insects!

 **Thanks to their size (big!) and their characteristic shape and claws, bear tracks are pretty easy to identify.**

Draw Your Own Track

Front

back

Animal tracks aren't the only ones you might find; people leave tracks too! Draw your track above. There are a few ways to do this: You can make a real track by stepping in wet sand or dirt (with your shoes on or off) and then you can draw the track. You can also trace your "front track" (your hands!) above.

> **Believe it or not, human "tracks" have helped police solve crimes.**

Make a Track Trap!

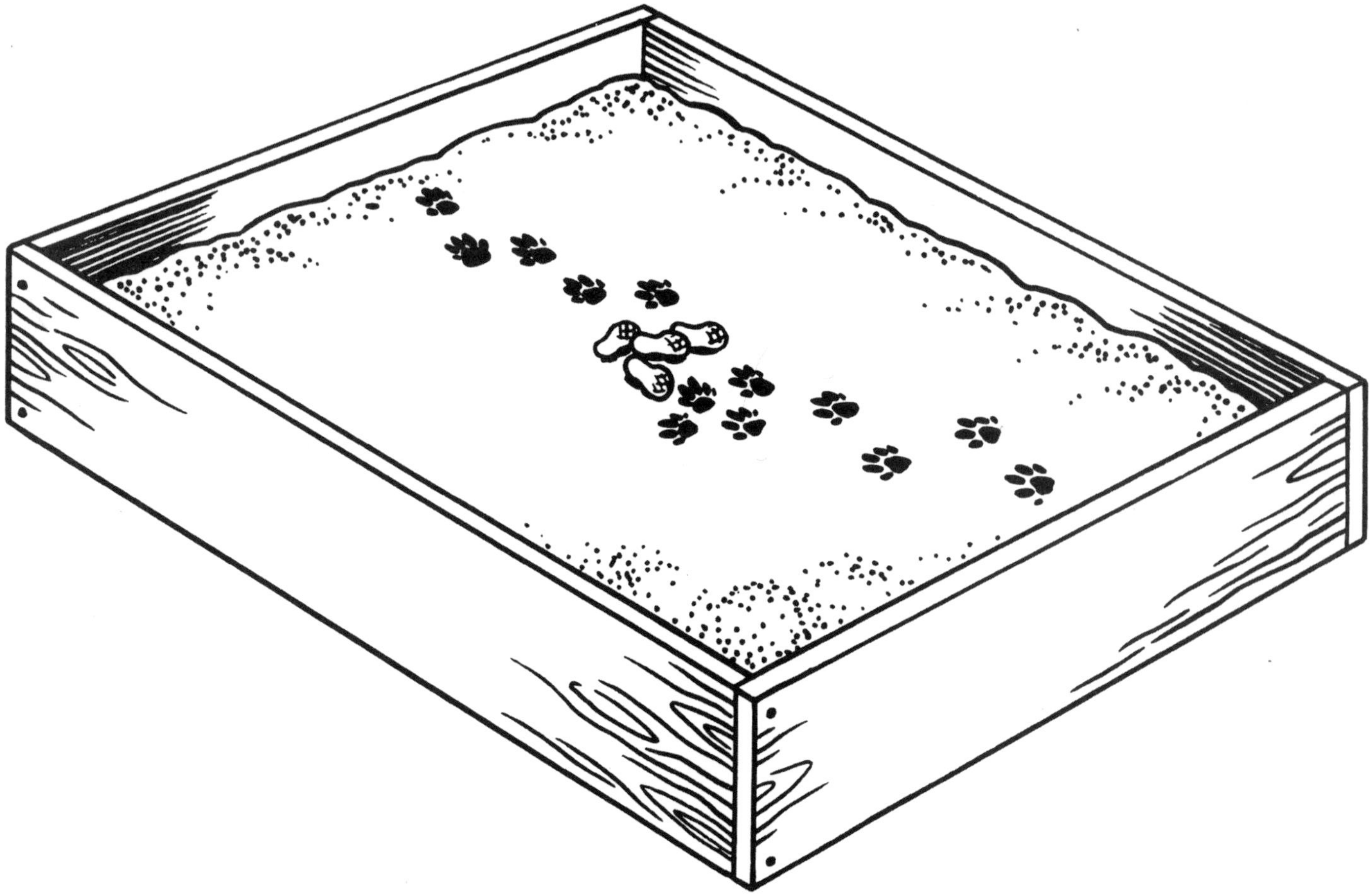

Want to get the animals to come to you? Build a track trap. All you need is an area of open ground (a garden or a sandbox). When you've found one, drag a heavy bag of garden soil to flatten the dirt (have a parent help). This makes it a perfect surface to retain tracks. Then, you just add some "bait" (peanuts or birdseed) and leave it out overnight. If you're lucky, you'll find animal tracks the next morning.

Once you've found your tracks, take pictures of the tracks the animals left behind. Can you identify them?

Preserve a Track with Plaster

You might think that tracks won't last very long, but that is not always true. You can actually preserve a track using plaster. Follow the instructions below to make your very own track cast!

You'll need

- A strip of plastic or cardboard that is larger than your track
- A paper clip
- Plaster of Paris
- A container for mixing

Directions

1. Remove any twigs or leaves around the track.

2. Use the plastic or cardboard to create a "wall" around the track. Use the paper clip to secure the ends together.

3. Add two parts plaster for every one part water (so if you use one cup of plaster, you should use a half cup of water).

4. Mix the plaster and water together until it is like pancake batter. Stir until the plaster isn't lumpy, usually at least a few minutes.

5. Pour the plaster inside your wall (but not directly onto the track), letting the plaster flow over the track gradually. Make sure you pour enough to cover the entire track to a depth of about ¾ of an inch.

6. Wait half an hour, then test the firmness of the plaster. Once it is hard enough, remove it by grabbing it at the edges. Wait a few days for it to dry completely.

Have an adult help you when creating a cast, as it can be a bit tricky. Once you have a cast, you can even frame it!

Tracking Journal

Where did you find it: _____

Did you find other signs of an animal (scat?): _____

Date: _____ How many tracks: _____ Track length: _____ Track width: _____

Animal you think made it: _____

One of the best ways to learn about animal tracks is to draw them! So when you a find a track, draw it here! Drawing tracks helps you memorize different track shapes, which helps make you even better at tracking.

 **Another great way to learn about tracks is to take a picture of the track, so be sure to bring along a camera!**

Field Guides, Playing Cards and Nature Journals

Once you've got an idea of what animal left behind the tracks you've found, it's time to hit the books! A good field guide is a must when you're out in the field. The following field guides are highly respected and great options for the beginning tracker.

Animal tracks playing cards are another great way to learn about animal tracks, as you can learn about animal tracks as you play a game of War or Go Fish. Playing cards work great as flashcards, too.

Finally, when you go tracking, bring along a nature journal. Keeping a nature journal forces you to pay attention to your surroundings, and it's a great way to get to know nature. A nature journal can be as simple as the tracking page in this book or as complex as a printed book specifically made for nature tracking.

Field Guides

Murie, Olaus J and Mark Elbroch. *Peterson Field Guide to Animal Tracks*: Third Edition. Boston: Houghton Mifflin Harcourt, 2005.

Elbroch, Mark and Eleanor Marks. *Bird Tracks & Sign : A Guide to North American Species*. Mechanicsburg: Stackpole Books, 2001.

Poppele, Jonathan. *Animal Tracks: Midwest Edition*. Cambridge: Adventure Publications, 2012.

Rezendes, Paul. *Tracking and the Art of Seeing: How to Read Animal Tracks and Sign*. New York: HarperCollins Reference, 1999.

Animal Tracks Playing Cards

Poppele, Jonathan. *Animal Tracks of the Midwest Playing Cards*. Cambridge: Adventure Publications, 2014.

Nature Journals

Brandt, DeAnna. *Nature Log Kids: A Kid's Journal to Record Their Nature Experiences*. Cambridge: Adventure Publications, 1998.

Answers

Page 3 Looking at a Track

The track is from a gray wolf.

Page 8 Animal Names Word Find

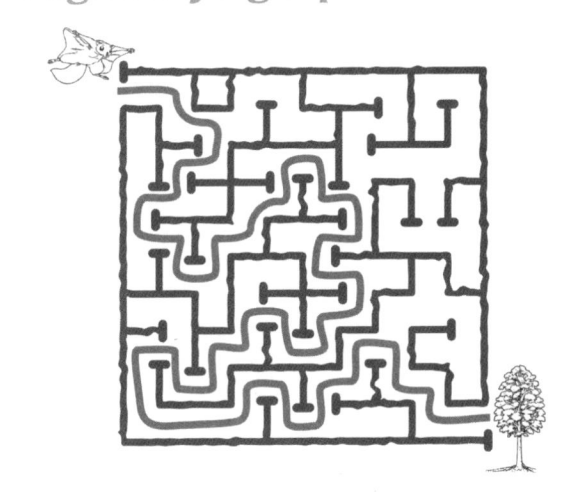

Bonus: Bear, Deer and Cougar

Page 9 Flying Squirrel Maze

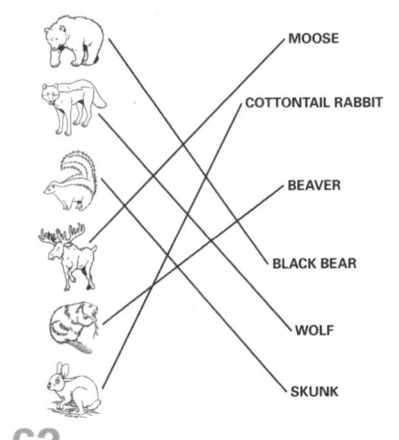

Page 10 Name the Animals

MOOSE

COTTONTAIL RABBIT

BEAVER

BLACK BEAR

WOLF

SKUNK

Page 11 Groups of Tracks

Porcupine: A
White-tailed Deer: D
Cottontail Rabbit: A

Page 18 Fill in the Blanks

Cat
Hare
Beaver
Porcupine
Muskrat
Lemming
Lynx
Badger

Page 23 Prairie Dog Maze

Page 26 Crack the Code

1. House cat
2. Prairie dog
3. Coyote
4. Bison
5. Beaver
6. House mouse
7. Moose
8. Skunk
9. Black bear
10. Cougar
Bonus: Fish

nswers

Page 28 Help the Beaver Reach Its Lodge!

Page 30 Gaits

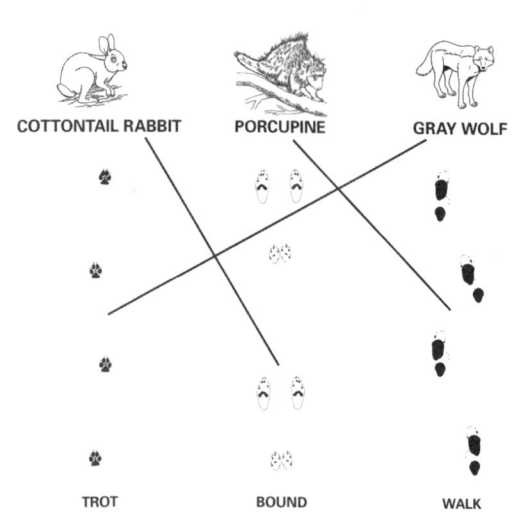

COTTONTAIL RABBIT	PORCUPINE	GRAY WOLF
TROT	BOUND	WALK

Page 34 Animal Names Crossword

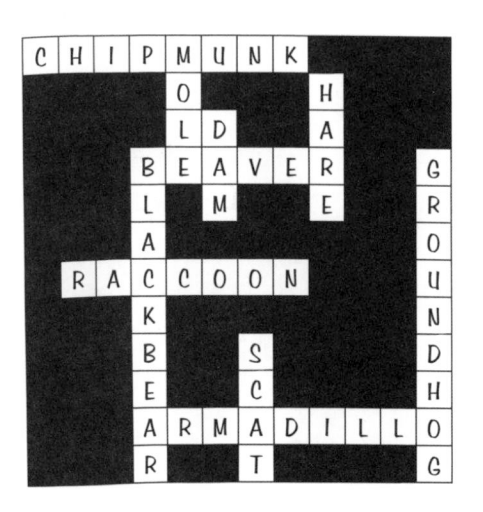

Page 37 How Many Mammals?

Page 39 Match the Tracks

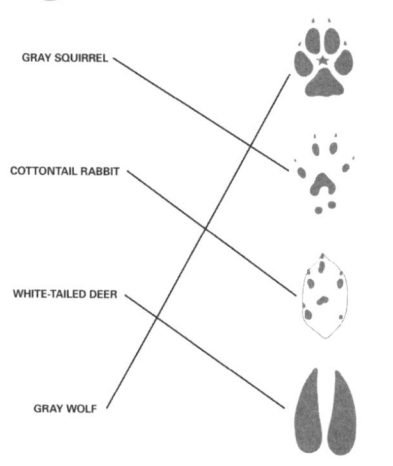

GRAY SQUIRREL
COTTONTAIL RABBIT
WHITE-TAILED DEER
GRAY WOLF

Page 48 Solve the Riddles!

A river, stream or brook
Bobcat
Prairie Dog

Answers

Page 51 What Made These Tiny Tracks?

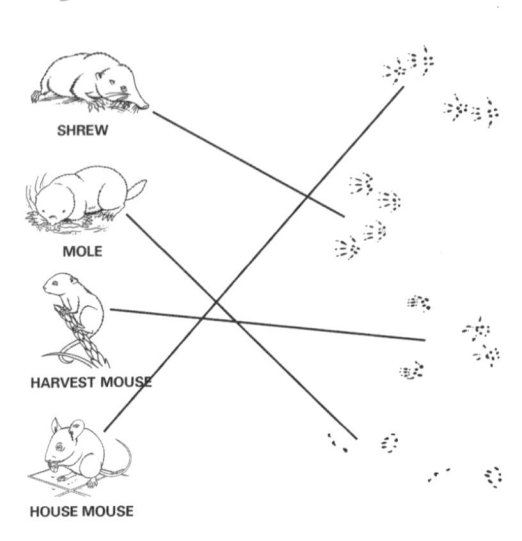

SHREW

MOLE

HARVEST MOUSE

HOUSE MOUSE

Page 53 What Made These Medium-Sized Tracks?

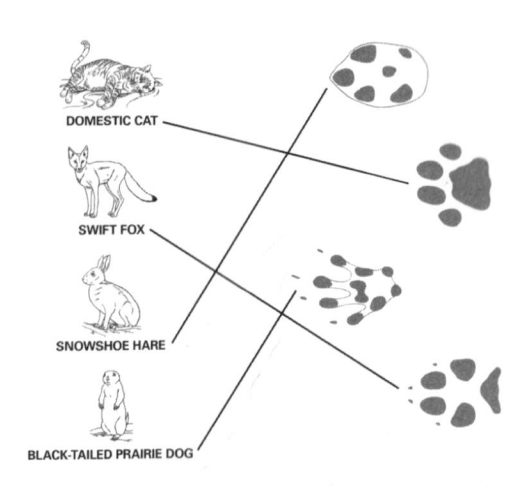

DOMESTIC CAT

SWIFT FOX

SNOWSHOE HARE

BLACK-TAILED PRAIRIE DOG

Page 55 What Made These Big Tracks?

1. Cougar
2. Bison
3. Elk
4. Black Bear

About the Author

Brett Ortler is the author of *The Fireflies Book*, *The Mosquito Book* and *Minnesota Trivia: Don'tcha Know!*. An editor at Adventure Publications, he has edited dozens of books, including many field guides and nature-themed books. His work appears widely, including in *Salon*, *The Good Men Project*, *The Nervous Breakdown*, *Living Ready* and in a number of other venues in print and online. He lives in the Twin Cities with his wife and their young children. For more, visit www.brettortler.com.